Angels
in your Presence

OMAR SULEIMAN

KUBE
PUBLISHING

In association with

INSTITUTE FOR ISLAMIC RESEARCH

Angels in Your Presence

First published in England by
Kube Publishing Ltd
Markfield Conference Centre
Ratby Lane, Markfield
Leicestershire, LE67 9SY
United Kingdom

Tel: +44 (0) 1530 249230

Website: www.kubepublishing.com
Email: info@kubepublishing.com

The author has directed that 100% of the royalties from the sale
of this book be donated to Yaqeen Institute, which is a non-profit
research institute, supporting their research and activities for the
global Muslim community.

Cataloguing-in-Publication Data is available from the
British Library.

ISBN 978-1-84774-150-9 Casebound
ISBN 978-1-84774-151-6 Ebook

Cover design, illustration and typesetting: Jannah Haque
Printed by: IMAK Ofset, Turkey.

Transliteration Guide

A brief guide to some of the letters and symbols used in the Arabic transliteration in this book.

th	ث	*ḥ*	ح	*dh*	ذ
ṣ	ص	*ḍ*	ض	*ṭ*	ط
ẓ	ظ	ʿ	ع	ʾ	ء

ā	آ ‍ـَا	*ī*	‍ـِي	*ū*	‍ـُو

 May the peace and blessings of Allah be upon him.

 May Allah be pleased with him

 May peace be upon him

Contents

Introduction...1

1. They've Got Your Back 3

2. Hold Your Pens...9

3. Fasting while Others Eat 13

4. Sleep Well...19

5. Switching Shifts...23

6. As You Step Outside 29

7. The Banner Above You 33

8. Responding to Your Haters...........................37

9. Your Brother's Honour..................................41

10. The Honour of Your Prophet ﷺ 45

11. Āmīn and for You as Well 49

12. The Best Supplication 55

13. Be Fair When You Judge 61

14. The Seeker of Knowledge 65

15. No Strings Attached 69

16. The Ultimate Healer 75

17. An Entourage of 70,000 81

18. When Your Loved Ones Are Dying 85

19. An Angel in Human Form 89

20. A Caller from Heaven's Gates............................95

21. The First Rows...99

22. The Friday Roll Book 105

23. From Prayer to Prayer 111

24. Struggling to Recite 115

25. Your Breath in Prayer......................................119

26. When Jibrīl  Descends.................................121

27. The Heavens Are Creaking 125

28. Praying Behind You 129

29. Gatherings of Remembrance...........................133

30. When Allah Loves You 137

Introduction

You are just a lump of flesh in the womb of your mother and then Allah sends an angel to you and the angel blows life into you at 120 days. The angel says, 'O my Lord! What is his sustenance? O my Lord! What are his deeds? O my Lord! What is his date of death?', and 'O my Lord! Is he amongst the blessed or the wretched?'.

You come out into this world and as you open your eyes, the first thing that happens is that the Devil (*Shayṭān*) pokes at you and says that you and I are going to have a long time together and that I will lead you astray. The angels fade into the background and you live this crazy life that proceeds so rapidly that even if you live seventy or eighty years, it's like the blink of an eye.

The Devil tries to tempt you to evil, and the angels try to call you to good. As you get older and you find yourself in the same state of vulnerability as when you came into this world, you look out and you see these angels coming down from the heavens with your shroud, and they call you back.

The angels say to the believers 'Come out to the pleasure of your Lord, come out to His forgiveness, come out to His mercy, we were with you through this entire journey and we will carry you throughout.' They take your soul from the body, you go to the grave and your questioners are two angels. You are raised on the Day of Judgment with an angel that drives you out and an angel that bears witness for or against you, and then you enter into Paradise where Angels enter upon you perpetually saying 'Peace be onto you for the patience that you had'.

In this book, we explore the various roles the angels play in our everyday lives and the blessings they bring from the invisible realm by the permission of our Creator.

They've Got Your Back

You see videos of incidents online, in which a person is walking on the street, unaware of the cars that are coming towards him and a huge truck which is about to collide into him. Suddenly it's as if an arm just pulls that truck away and it goes in a completely different direction and that person is unharmed. On the other hand, you see someone who is involved in a freak accident. For instance, a person who is jogging on the beach is suddenly hit by a vehicle or something moving, and it is like witnessing a divine decree in precision. You witnessed that perfect *Qadar* of Allah (*glorified and exalted is He*).

Now relate that to your own self. You're driving on the highway and you are saved from a car accident. You're doing something that distracts you, and in that moment of distraction something horrible is about to happen and then you see what happened around you and you say, '*Subḥān Allāh*, Allah protected me'. Another example are those that have seen their children fall, knowing that if they had fallen slightly differently, they would have hit the back of their head and it could have been catastrophic.

All these things that we have witnessed in our lives speak to the overwhelming power of Allah (*glorified and exalted is He*), but they have something to do with the angels as well. Allah (*glorified and exalted is He*) says, لَهُ مُعَقِّبَاتٌ مِنْ بَيْنِ يَدَيْهِ وَمِنْ خَلْفِهِ يَحْفَظُونَهُ مِنْ أَمْرِ اللهِ that every single person has a guardian angel behind him and in front of him that protect him, by the Decree of Allah (*glorified and exalted is He*).

That concept requires a lot of reflection. First and foremost, it is a testament to the mercy of Allah (*glorified and exalted is He*). We are always so paranoid about the devils (*shayāṭīn*) and the Jinn being everywhere,

*A*llah has
set up guardian angels
for each person, and
the only time a person
is harmed is when
those angels are told
to stand down by
Allah's Decree.

but each of us has only one *shayṭān* and four angels
assigned to them. Everything else that is invited into
one's life of angels or devils is invited as a result of
one's good or bad deeds, but every single person has,
proportionately speaking, four angels that are with
them and just one devil that whispers and tempts.

Of the four angels, two of them protect you and the
other two angels record your deeds, but what do these
guardian angels do? What role do they play in your
life? They are always with you. They're with you during
the day, they're with you when you sleep at night, they
are with you for the most significant and insignificant
moments of divine decree within your life. Mujahid
(*Allah's mercy be upon him*) said that your guardian
angels protect you from any wild animal, from any
riding animal, from any beast or person that wants to
harm you and even from النَّمْلُ فِي أُذُنِكَ, 'an ant in your
ear'. If the decree is not upon you to be harmed, the
angels will shoo away those bugs and push away those
harmful objects that are coming your way, in order to
protect you.

'Alī ibn Abī Ṭālib (*Allah's mercy be upon him*) said that when he was told that the tribe of Murad were planning to attack him, he replied, 'they cannot harm me with anything unless Allah (*glorified and exalted is He*) has decreed it. For Allah (*glorified and exalted is He*) has set up guardian angels for each person, and the only time a person is harmed is when those angels are told to stand down'. That's when Ibn 'Abbās (*Allah's mercy be upon him*) said, 'Out of obedience to Allah (*glorified and exalted is He*), those angels will protect you and will be there for you, and they will only move out of the way when Allah (*glorified and exalted is He*) decrees otherwise'. This is a powerful concept on an individual level because it reminds us about the story of the Prophet (*peace be upon him*) who was protected from his enemies by Jibrīl (*peace be upon him*) or the hundreds of angels that were sent down to protect the Muslims in the Battle of Badr.

During the battle, the Muslims could even see that their enemies were being thrown off their horses, and could hear the sound of the whip cracking on someone, but they could not see who was doing it. There is also the example of the Prophet's warning about the end of times when the Dajjāl will try to enter Madīnah and find angels guarding its gates from all directions.

Ibn ʿAbbās' (*Allah's mercy be upon him*) statement applies to us all. Each of us is protected by these angels that are in front of us and behind us and the only time they step aside is when Allah (*glorified and exalted is He*) decrees that harm is coming to us, and that harm is what is assigned to us in the womb, a decree also written by an angel. When the decree of death comes our way, the angels will move aside, only for our soul to be transferred to another group of angels with the shroud of either Paradise or Hellfire.

2) Hold Your Pens

The Prophet (*peace be upon him*) warned: إِذَا ذُكِّرْتُمْ بِاللهِ فَانْتَهُوا If you are reminded of Allah (*glorified and exalted is He*) when you are about to commit a sin, do not ignore your conscience (*taqwa*). Rather than saying, 'I'm already halfway through the sin or I'm already at the point of committing it, I may as well continue and then worry about repentance later', stop yourself, because you are one of those people of which Allah (*glorified and exalted is He*) says: تَذَكَّرُوا فَإِذَا هُم مُّبْصِرُونَ After they've been touched by the whisper of the Devil, they wake up and suddenly they can see. That is the best-case scenario—that you are about to commit the sin, but you are stopped from doing so, but what if you have already sinned?

You feel dirty and impure, regretful and remorseful, especially if it is the first time you are committing that sin and you have not become desensitised to it. What you do in those moments is going to decide whether that sin becomes a means of bringing you back to Allah (*glorified and exalted is He*) or it becomes a habit that takes you down the path of the *Shayṭān* perpetually. It is in reference to moments like this that the Prophet (*peace be upon him*) talks about a very unique way that we interact with the angels that are recording our deeds. وَإِنَّ عَلَيْكُمْ لَحَافِظِينَ كِرَامًا كَاتِبِينَ These noble angels have been commanded by Allah (*glorified and exalted is He*) to record everything we say and do. مَا يَلْفِظُ مِن قَوْلٍ إِلَّا لَدَيْهِ رَقِيبٌ عَتِيدٌ There is not a single word or expression that you utter that is not written down by the angels. Al-Sufyān (*Allah's mercy be upon him*) said that when a person is about to commit a good deed, their soul emits a beautiful scent of musk and when they are about to commit a sin the soul emits a nasty stench. As the angels write, they have a sense of when you are about to commit a good deed or if you are about to commit a sin.

However, there is one exception. Allah's Messenger (*peace be upon him*) tells us, 'When a person first commits a sin, Allah (*glorified and exalted is He*) commands the angel on the left to hold his pen for six hours'. In this context, an hour does not mean sixty minutes but six periods of time. If that person repents within those six periods of time, then Allah (*glorified and exalted is He*) commands the angels to record a good deed in place of a sin. The Prophet (*peace be upon him*) said, 'A sin is written down as one sin if a person actually commits it but the good deed, at a minimum, is written as ten good deeds, up to 700, up to whatever Allah (*glorified and exalted is He*) decrees'. It was also said that even if the sin was written down: التَّائِبُ مِنَ الذَّنْبِ كَمَنْ لَا ذَنْبَ لَهُ The one who repents from the sin is like the one who never committed the sin in the first place. This shows that Allah (*glorified and exalted is He*) always leaves the door of repentance open to us. What does this signify in the unique situation where an angel is told not to document the sin? It means that on your records, not only will that sin be absent, but that you will instead have the good deed of seeking forgiveness from Allah (*glorified and exalted is He*) recorded a minimum of ten times.

This does not apply to a person who intends to sin because they feel reassured that if they repent within six hours, they will not be answerable for it. It refers to someone who, following a rash mistake, makes the sincere intention to return to Allah (*glorified and exalted is He*). The mercy of your Lord (*glorified and exalted is He*) is such, that even as the angels on the left and right of you are recording your deeds at all times, Allah (*glorified and exalted is He*) shows leniency through the one on the left and says, 'Hold your pen and see if my servant will turn back to Me, see if he will wake up in the midst of that moment and decide that this is not something he ever wants to do again'. And verily a sin that brings a person back to Allah (*glorified and exalted is He*) is better than a good deed that takes him away.

3) Fasting While Others Eat

Almost every Muslim who lives as a minority has experienced a moment in which they are fasting and people are eating around them. Whether that moment occurs in a school cafeteria where all the other students are having lunch or whether it is at a work meeting or function where their colleagues are enjoying the catering, it can be a challenging experience. However, those moments are in fact some of the most blessed in our lives.

There are several times in the day that the angels pray for a person (also known as sending *Ṣalawāt*). The Prophet (*peace be upon him*) talked about *suḥūr*, the pre-dawn meal one has before Fajr. He advised against

The suḥūr, the pre-dawn meal before fasting, is one of the key moments in the day when the angels pray for a person, even before the fast has began.

neglecting *suḥūr* as it is one of the key moments in the day that the angels pray for a person, even if that person is only consuming a few dates or taking a sip of water. That means that the angels are praying for you before your fast has even began.

Another key moment for receiving *Ṣalawāt* is when you are fasting around those who are not observing that fast. The Prophet (*peace be upon him*) said, 'A person who is fasting around people that are eating, the angels will pray for that person until those people have had their fill'. *Subḥān Allāh!* This is not referring to non-Muslims who are eating and drinking around you because they do not observe siyam, but to a person who is just not required to fast for that day. Take the example of Umm ʿUmārah (*Allah's mercy be upon her*) who was observing a voluntary fast in proximity of the Prophet (*peace be upon him*) who was not fasting and so the Prophet (*peace be upon him*) gave her that reward.

Imagine then, the reward for fasting around someone who is eating and drinking because they don't consider the fast to be obligatory. Here we see the element of being a stranger (*ghurbah*) come into play. You have been singled out for the observance of the fast because you have been singled out for your adherence to this beautiful faith of Islam, and so the reward awarded to you will be even greater. When you are in those moments, revel in the prayer of the angels as they are seeking forgiveness for you throughout that entire period.

At night comes the opportunity to offer a *du'a'* for others to receive the blessings of the angels. The beautiful supplication of the Prophet (*peace be upon him*) taught us that when someone serves you iftar and you actually break your fast, you respond with these words:

أَفْطَرَ عِنْدَكُمُ الصَّائِمُونَ وَأَكَلَ طَعَامَكُمُ الأَبْرَارُ وَصَلَّتْ عَلَيْكُمُ الْمَلاَئِكَةُ

'May the fasting ones break their fast with you, (وَأَكَلَ طَعَامَكُمُ الأَبْرَارُ), may the pious eat their food with you or take part in your food, (وَصَلَّتْ عَلَيْكُمُ الْمَلاَئِكَةُ), and may the angels send their prayers upon you'. Therefore, the angels pray for you throughout the day as you are observing your fast, they pray for you when you take your pre-morning meal and they pray for you when other people around you are eating as you are fasting.

Not only that, but they then pray for those that serve you food at the time of iftar and you acknowledge that through your supplications and through your *du'ā'*.

The Prophet ﷺ said that a person who is fasting around people who are eating, the angels will pray for that person until those people have had their fill.

4) *Sleep Well*

When you are in bed, tired, the last thing you may feel like doing is reciting all of the remembrances (*adhkār*) that the Prophet (*peace be upon him*) recommended or getting up to perform ablution (*wuḍū'*) thereby going to sleep in a state of purity, as the Prophet (*peace be upon him*) did. Instead, you may feel tempted to check your social media or send a few text messages, or just go straight to sleep. However, there are so many *aḥādīth* that talk about the angels' involvement in your going to sleep and the effect it will have on the next morning and there is so much you can do in those last moments before sleep to invite their blessings.

The Prophet (*peace be upon him*) said, 'Every night as you go to your bed an angel and a devil come to you and they start to prompt you'. This is in accordance with another *ḥadīth* which states that, 'Throughout the day the *Shayṭān* whispers to you and prompts you towards evil and promises you poverty and tragedy and the angel prompts you towards good and to the promise of Allah (*glorified and exalted is He*)', and so you are constantly pulled between those influences.

Regarding night time, the Prophet (*peace be upon him*) said, 'In those moments an angel comes to you and says, اخْتِمْ بِخَيْرٍ، اخْتِمْ بِخَيْرٍ، اخْتِمْ بِخَيْرٍ, end your night well, end your night well, end your night well and the devil comes and says, end your night in evil, end your night in evil, end your night in evil'. This could be a bad word, thought or exchange and it will undermine all your good deeds as actions are judged by their endings, إِنَّمَا الأَعْمَالُ بِالْخَوَاتِيمِ.

At night when you sleep, it is اَلَمَوتُ الأَصْغَرُ, your minor death. Your soul returns to Allah *(glorified and exalted is He)* and there is no certainty that you will wake up the next morning so just as you live your life and it is those last moments before death that count so much, such is also the case, when you are going to sleep. Therefore, heed the words of the angels who say اخْتِمْ بِخَيْرٍ. End your night with remembrance of Allah (*glorified and exalted is He*), end your night reading Qur'an, end your night with good things.

There are so many good things that we should do at night that are mentioned by the Messenger of Allah (*peace be upon him*) and they do involve the angels. To begin with, when a person performs ablution so that Allah (*glorified and exalted is He*) may purify them at night, an angel is sent down to spend the entire night at their head and that angel says, اللَّهُمَّ اِغْفِرْ لِعَبْدِكَ كَمَا بَاتَ طَاهِرًا, 'O Allah! Forgive your servant, as he went to sleep in a state of *wuḍū'* (purification)'. That prayer for your forgiveness will continue throughout the entire night just because you took those moments to purify yourself before sleep.

The Prophet (*peace be upon him*) also advises us to recite *Āyat al-Kursī* as Allah (*glorified and exalted is He*) will then send an angel that will stand guard for us and protect us from any devil that may approach us at night. Therefore, just by making *wuḍū'*, you have an angel that seeks forgiveness for you throughout the night and just by reciting *Āyat al-Kursī,* you have an angel that stands guard for you until the morning. In each case you have ended your night well. If you die that night, you return to Allah (*glorified and exalted is He*) in a state of remembrance as opposed to in a state of whatever it is that you are doing before going to sleep and if you wake up in the morning, you wake up already oriented towards Allah (*glorified and exalted is He*).

5) *Switching Shifts*

We have already established that remembering Allah (*glorified and exalted is He*), performing ablution and reciting *Āyat al-Kursī* before sleep invites the angels to protect us and seek forgiveness on our behalf. If you meet Allah (*glorified and exalted is He*) in that state, you need not fear because you left this world in a state of remembrance and in a state of purification, but how does this affect the next day when you wake up?

Allah (*glorified and exalted is He*) mentions in the Qur'an: إِنَّ قُرْآنَ الْفَجْرِ كَانَ مَشْهُودًا That the Qur'an that is recited at the time of Fajr is witnessed by the angels who are switching shifts. To clarify, you have the angels of

You have
the angels of the
night protecting you
and asking Allah to
forgive you and the
angels of the daytime,
both guarding and
recording you.

the night protecting you and asking Allah (*glorified and exalted is He*) to forgive you and the angels of the daytime, both guarding and recording you. The Prophet (*peace be upon him*) explained that those angels change shifts at Fajr time and at 'Aṣr time. This is when Allah (*glorified and exalted is He*) gathers them around you as you recite the Qur'an.

This is also connected to the congregational Fajr prayer, where you wake up, طَيِّبَ النَّفْسِ، نَشِيطًا طَيِّبَ النَّفْسِ, energetic and in good spirits, with a longing towards Allah (*glorified and exalted is He*), and then you make your way to the congregational prayer. All of the angels of each person at the prayer, those that work the morning shift as well as those that work the evening shift, are gathered around, listening to the recitation of the Qur'an. When Allah (*glorified and exalted is He*) asks those angels, 'How did you find my servants?' they reply, تَرَكْنَاهُمْ وَهُمْ يُصَلُّونَ، وَأَتَيْنَاهُمْ وَهُم يُصَلُّونَ 'We left them while they were in a state of prayer, and we came to them while they were in a state of prayer'.

The Qur'an recitation at Fajr is supposed to be the longest recitation of the Qur'an, ensuring we begin our day fully connected to Allah (*glorified and exalted is He*). When the Prophet (*peace be upon him*) was asked about a person who sleeps through the night and then wakes up after sunrise, missing the Fajr recitation, he said of that person, بَالَ الشَّيْطَانُ فِي أُذُنِهِ, that the devil urinated in their ears. This is very different to the person on whom angels wait, for whom the angels seek forgiveness and about whom they report back favourably to Allah (*glorified and exalted is He*).

There are also implications for the remembrances that we make. The Prophet (*peace be upon him*) said, سَدِّدُوا وَقَارِبُوا، وَاغْدُوا وَرُوحُوا، وَشَيْءٌ مِنَ الدُّلْجِةِ، وَالقَصْدَ الْقَصْدَ تَبْلُغُوا 'Be sincere and moderate in your good deeds. سَدِّدُوا وَقَارِبُوا Do your best, aim for perfection but know that you have to be moderate in that pursuit of perfection. وَاغْدُوا وَرُوحُوا and use the time after Fajr until the sunrise and use the evening between ʿAṣr and Maghrib to get ahead'. Ibn Rajab (*Allah's mercy be upon him*) said that the Prophet (*peace be upon him*) gave us the method (*manhaj*) for how we perform our deeds. We set the standard of perfection, but we moderately pursue that perfection. Then he mentioned الغَدْوَةُ والرَّوْحَةُ which is the morning time between Fajr and sunrise, and the evening time

The Prophet ﷺ explained that the angels change shifts at Fajr time and at 'Aṣr time. That is when Allah gathers them around you as you recite the Qur'an.

between 'Aṣr and Maghrib. The Prophet (*peace be upon him*) gave us the best of times أَفْضَلُ الأَوْقَاتِ. If we make use of those times that the angels are gathered around us as they are switching shifts, they will find us in the state of remembrance.

The Prophet (*peace be upon him*) also said بُورِكَ لِأُمَّتِي فِي بُكُورِهَا, that my nation is blessed in its mornings. Start your morning with Fajr, with recitation, and why not get a head start on your day in terms of your halal worldly pursuits as well? One of the companions (*Allah's mercy be upon him*) took the advice of the Prophet (*peace be upon him*) and started work earlier than everyone else each day and he always found himself to be ahead of others in his work. The early morning is a truly blessed time so use those moments during which both the night-time and day-time angels are gathered round you to start your day well.

6 As You Step Outside

When we open the front door to look outside, we usually have an idea of what form the day will take. Based on the weather or how we are feeling, we predict whether it will be a good or bad day, but there is one thing we should do in that precise moment to begin the day the right way.

The Prophet (*peace be upon him*) gave us a beautiful remembrance to start off our day as we go outside of our home. As you are about to step out into the world, the two angels that are protecting you approach and at that moment you should say:

بِسْمِ اللهِ تَوَكَّلْتُ عَلَى اللهِ وَلاَ حَوْلَ وَلاَ قُوَّةَ اِلاَّ بِاللهِ

It's not a complicated form of remembrance. بِسْمِ اللهِ, in the name of Allah (*glorified and exalted is He*), تَوَكَّلْتُ عَلَى اللهِ, I put my trust in Allah (*glorified and exalted is He*), وَلاَ حَوْلَ وَلاَ قُوَّةَ اِلاَّ بِاللهِ that there is no power or might except that which belongs to Allah (*glorified and exalted is He*).

The Prophet (*peace be upon him*) said, 'When you say those words as you exit your home and enter the world outside, those angels respond to you. As you say *Bismillāh*, they say هُدِيتَ, in the name of Allah you've been guided, and when you say تَوَكَّلْتُ عَلَى اللهِ, I've put my full trust in Allah (*glorified and exalted is He*), they say وَكُفِيتَ, you've been defended against anyone that is going to try to harm you. And when you say وَلاَ حَوْلَ وَلاَ قُوَّةَ اِلاَّ بِاللهِ, there is no power or might except which belongs to Allah (*glorified and exalted is He*), they say وُقِيتَ, and you've been protected from all harm for the day'. At this point, the two devils that arrive to attack you ask one another, 'what can we do with a person who's been guided, defended, and protected?' They know they have been rendered powerless and so they abandon you for the rest of the day.

These words of remembrance also played a crucial part
in the life of ʿUmar ibn al-Khaṭṭāb (*Allah's mercy be
upon him*). He was so pure that he did not just utter
the words, بِسْمِ اللهِ تَوَكَّلْتُ عَلَى اللهِ وَلاَ حَوْلَ وَلاَ قُوَّةَ اِلاَّ بِاللهِ, he
lived them. ʿUmar (*Allah's mercy be upon him*) had such
a desire to be guided that the Prophet (*peace be upon
him*) said that he was naturally drawn to the truth
because the angels would speak to him (*Muhaddathun*).
Therefore, his intuition matched divine guidance and
he had such trust in Allah (*glorified and exalted is He*)
that he couldn't be harmed by anyone else. The power
of ʿUmar (*Allah's mercy be upon him*) came from his
belief in the power of Allah (*glorified and exalted is He*)
and the Prophet (*peace be upon him*) said that when
ʿUmar ibn al-Khaṭṭāb (*Allah's mercy be upon him*) took a
path, the Devil would take another path to avoid him.

How do we bring that kind of blessing into our own
lives? As you are entering into the world, say,
بِسْمِ اللهِ تَوَكَّلْتُ عَلَى اللهِ وَلاَ حَوْلَ وَلاَ قُوَّةَ اِلاَّ بِاللهِ, 'In the name
of Allah (*glorified and exalted is He*), I've put my trust in
Allah (*glorified and exalted is He*) and there is no power
or might except that which is with Allah (*glorified
and exalted is He*)' and the angels will guide you and

protect you throughout the day. Meanwhile, the devils, knowing you are guarded, will avoid you just as they avoided 'Umar (*Allah's mercy be upon him*).

The Banner Above You

7

When discussing intentions, the Prophet (*peace be upon him*) said, 'No person leaves the home except that there is a devil and an angel both waiting with a banner in their hand. If a person does or intends what Allah (*glorified and exalted is He*) loves for the day, the angel follows that person with a banner over his head for the rest of the day and that person does not relinquish the banner until they return home'. There is no remembrance (*dhikr*) that can protect you from bad intentions and you cannot utter a remembrance while harbouring bad intentions and expect to be rewarded.

The remembrance must be an expression of what you long for and desire in your heart, as it was with ʿUmar ibn al-Khaṭṭāb (*Allah's mercy be upon him*).

As you open your door to the outside and you say, بِسْمِ اللهِ تَوَكَّلْتُ عَلَى اللهِ وَلاَ حَوْلَ وَلاَ قُوَّةَ اِلاَّ بِاللهِ what is your intention for the world? If you desire to stay engaged with that which is beloved to Allah (*glorified and exalted is He*), an angel carries a banner declaring your love for Allah (*glorified and exalted is He*) over your head for the entire day. However, if your intentions are bad, a devil will carry a banner over your head declaring that you wish to carry out evil in the world today.

Another narration relays that the Prophet (*peace be upon him*) said, 'No human being leaves the house except that there is an angel holding reins (*hakamah*) over their head. If they are humble, Allah (*glorified and exalted is He*) tells the angels to raise those reins, but if they are arrogant, then Allah (*glorified and exalted is He*) tells the angels to lower their reins'. If we read this in conjunction with the Prophet's words, 'Whoever humbles themselves to their Lord, Allah (*glorified and exalted is He*) elevates them', we understand that when the angels are said to be raising your head, they are in fact raising your ranks. It is not a physical lift, but a spiritual one that is pleasing to Allah (*glorified and exalted is He*). In the same way, when the angels are said to lower the reins, it is a metaphor for the humiliation that one who shows pride in the sight of Allah (*glorified and exalted is He*) must face.

Although they differ slightly, both narrations are profound in that they speak to the intentions of our heart. So, as you leave your home each day and you state your remembrance, do not just mouth the words. Renew your intention to do good in the world and refresh it throughout the day so you can maintain the humility that is beloved of Allah (*glorified and exalted is He*). In return, you will be counted amongst those that proceed under the banner of His love and you will be raised in honour by the angel that He sends to elevate you.

As you leave your home each day, renew your intention to do good in the world and refresh it throughout the day so you can maintain the humility that is beloved to Allah.

Responding to Your Haters

8

We have already touched upon the idea that the angels will elevate us when we humble ourselves before Allah (*glorified and exalted is He*) but how should we respond with humility when faced with someone who behaves with arrogance and pride? Imam Ghazālī said, 'The greatest test of حُسْنُ الخُلُقِ, of good character, is how a person deals with someone with سُوءُ الخُلُقِ, bad character'. That is when the flaws of the tongue come out, when the flaws of character, and the flaws of the heart manifest themselves. It may be a colleague who is disrespectful towards you, a stranger in the street, or someone who insults you on social media. When faced with confrontation, how should you behave in a way that is pleasing to Allah (*glorified and exalted is He*)?

We can find the answer in the story of the Prophet (*peace be upon him*) and Abū Bakr (*Allah's mercy be upon him*) who were approached by a man who began to insult them. The Prophet (*peace be upon him*) responded with patience, as he always did, choosing not to respond in like manner. However, Abū Bakr (*Allah's mercy be upon him*) who loved the Prophet (*peace be upon him*) more than he loved himself, was witnessing those insults and finally could no longer be silent in the face of such an attack and he made a riposte. As soon as he did so, the Prophet (*peace be upon him*) rose to his feet and walked away from him. Abū Bakr (*Allah's mercy be upon him*) was afraid that he may have offended the Prophet (*peace be upon him*) and so he approached him and asked, 'O Messenger of Allah, are you upset with me? Is it something that I did?' The Prophet's reply was, 'Before we responded to those insults, Allah (*glorified and exalted is He*) had sent an angel from the heavens, and that angel was responding to everything that was being said to us. As soon as you opened your mouth, the angel left and a devil came and sat in its place. I did not want to sit in the presence of that devil'. *Subḥān Allāh!* Consider that statement. An angel will be sent down specifically to respond on your behalf, but as soon as you reply, that angel is replaced with a devil who incites you towards more bad behaviour. That is why the Prophet (*peace be upon him*) said, 'Strength is not how you overcome another person, strength is actually how you overcome yourself', الَّذِي يَمْلِكُ نَفْسَهُ عِنْدَ الغَضَبِ. Retorts and reactions are usually driven by a sense of pride and it is when you give in to your pride you hand over control to the devil. That is why you can say things in a fit of rage, that you otherwise would never say.

Controlling yourself, by yielding to the angel to respond on your behalf is what the Prophet (*peace be upon him*) taught us. When you do that, 'not only do you cause the *Shayṭān* to miss you with his arrows, but you also cause him to waste his arrows' (Ibn al-Qayyim). In other words, you are causing the devil to despair that he cannot lower your character. This is when the angel raises your reins, thereby raising your station in the sight of Allah (*glorified and exalted is He*).

Someone approached Wahb ibn Munabbih and said to him, 'So and so said this about you'. Wahb ibn Munabbih replied, 'Did *Shayṭān* not find a postman other than you? Stop acting like the *Shayṭān's* postman.

I'm okay, I'm good, the angels will take care of me because I said بِسْمِ اللهِ تَوَكَّلْتُ عَلَى اللهِ، وَلاَ حَوْلَ وَلَا قُوَّةَ إِلَّا بِاللهِ I put my trust in Allah (*glorified and exalted is He*) and I was told that I would be defended, فَسَيَكْفِيْكَهُمُ اللهُ, and Allah (*glorified and exalted is He*) will surely suffice me through those angels that He has sent. I do not feel the need to denigrate myself, by responding in like manner, so I remain dignified in the face of insult and in that process, Allah (*glorified and exalted is He*) honours me, 'بِإِذْنِ اللهِ تَعَالَى.

With His permission, we ask Allah (*glorified and exalted is He*) to honour us all.

9 Your Brother's Honour

In the previous chapter, we learnt that we should not respond in like manner to those who are disrespectful towards us, but this begs the question: what type of society are we creating if we allow people to be insulted, and we ask them to not respond on their own behalf? What type of imbalance occurs when people are expected to tolerate bad behaviour? The answer to that is, Allah (*glorified and exalted is He*) tasks us with responding on behalf of other people, especially where someone is absent when they are being denigrated.

The Prophet (*peace be upon him*) said, 'Whoever defends their brother or their sister in their absence,

رَدَّ اللّٰهُ وَجْهَهُ عَنِ النَّارِ يَوْمَ القِيَامَةِ, Allah (*glorified and exalted is He*) will remove the Fire from that person's face on the Day of Judgment'. This means that a Muslim who is expected to respond to an attack on themselves with humility and self-control, should not tolerate their brother or sister being insulted and disparaged. In defending the character of their brother or sister, that person is drawing, not on a sense of pride, but of honour (*ghīrah*) and what that does is create a culture in which bad behaviour like backbiting and slander will always be challenged. The analogy between the face and reputation is one that is used throughout the Qur'an and the Sunnah of the Prophet (*peace be upon him*) and by defending another's honour, your face will be protected from the Fire in the next life just as you have protected another from humiliation in this life.

In another beautiful, authentic *ḥadīth*, the Prophet (*peace be upon him*) says, 'Whoever defends his brother or sister in their absence when they are being insulted, Allah (*glorified and exalted is He*) will appoint an angel that will defend their flesh over the bridge (*ṣirāt*) on the Day of Judgment'. Once again, we are provided with an example of the angels protecting us when we act in a way that is pleasing to Allah (*glorified and exalted is He*). However, for those of us who choose the way of the Devil, the Prophet's warning is clear, 'whoever disgraces his brother or sister will be suspended over the bridge over Hellfire on the Day of Judgment until they are interrogated for what they have done'.

Subḥān Allāh! On the one hand you have someone who defended their brother and sister and is therefore protected from the Fire by an angel on the Day of Judgment and on the other, you have the person who has disgraced, taunted or slandered someone. They are forced to face the fire of Hell until revenge is taken for the bad deeds they have committed against their brethren. If we refer back to the *ḥadīth* which recounts how an angel responded on behalf of the Prophet (*peace be upon him*) and Abū Bakr (*Allah's mercy be upon him*) when they were verbally attacked, we understand that those of us who defend the honour of another are not only protected by the angels, but take on the role of the angel in guarding the one who is under attack. In doing so, we become angelic in character just as we seek to be like the angels in our worship.

Those who defend the honour of others are not only protected by the angels, but they take on the role of the angel in guarding the one who is under attack.

10 The Honour of Your Prophet ﷺ

No person who loves Allah (*glorified and exalted is He*) and His Messenger (*peace be upon him*) can be completely unaffected by the way the Prophet (*peace be upon him*) has been drawn, ridiculed and portrayed (particularly in Western imagery) to look like the negative stereotype of a Muslim man; barbaric, angry, regressive and violent. The result of this is that all Muslims, especially Muslim men, are seen through this negative lens.

How then, as someone who loves the Rasūl Allāh (*peace be upon him*) should you respond when he is being insulted? If you allow yourself to be led by your raw emotions, you are submitting to the very image that has been used to denigrate the Prophet (*peace be upon him*). Your desire to defend him should be in accordance with his Sunnah. You want to defend him in such a way whereby you make the substantive arguments that are needed to be made to cast away those suspicions, those aspersions, that have been cast upon him (*peace be upon him*), yet at the same time, you also don't want to mould to that image because that's what they're trying to do: portray him in a certain negative way.

Previously, we discussed the reward that awaits the Muslim who shields their brother or sister from slander when they are not present to defend themselves. What then is the reward of protecting the Prophet (*peace be upon him*) in his absence? One does not want to defend the Messenger of Allah (*peace be upon him*) in a way that will only cause him to be further disparaged. Therefore, our approach must be holistic. There is no act of worship more beautiful and beloved to the angels than defending the Prophet (*peace be upon him*). That is why the angels of Badr who fought alongside his special companions when no one else would, are so revered. When Jibrīl (*peace be upon him*) asked him, 'How do you view the veterans of Badr amongst you?'

(meaning human beings) the Prophet (*peace be upon him*) replied, 'They are the best of us'. To this, Jibrīl (*peace be upon him*) said, 'The angels who served on that day are considered the best of us'.

There is also the example of Hassān ibn Thabit (*Allah's mercy be upon him*). He was a poet sent by the Prophet's enemies to lampoon him. However, when he saw the Prophet (*peace be upon him*), he could say nothing but words of beauty about his appearance and his character. Hassān ibn Thābit (*Allah's mercy be upon him*) became Muslim and responded to the enemies of Rasul Allah (*peace be upon him*) on his behalf. In fact, Hassān (*Allah's mercy be upon him*) was so talented in doing this, a pulpit (*minbar*) was built for him in the *Masjid* of the Prophet. On more than one occasion the Prophet (*peace be upon him*) said, 'Jibrīl (*peace be upon him*) is with Hassān (*Allah's mercy be upon him*)' and would even tell him, اهْجُ المُشْرِكِينَ، فَإِنَّ جِبْرِيلَ مَعَكَ, 'Satirize them because Jibrīl (*peace be upon him*) is with you'.

Some of the scholars connect that to a verse in *Sūrah al-Ḥashr* where Allah (*glorified and exalted is He*) talks about the believers who love the Prophet (*peace be upon him*) more than themselves, وَأَيَّدَهُمْ بِرُوحٍ مِنْهُ, 'And Allah supports them with a spirit from Him'. The majority of the scholars say, رُوحٌ مِنْهُ refers to the spirit of the power of Allah (*glorified and exalted is He*) rather than رُوحُ القُدُس , Jibrīl (*peace be upon him*) being the Holy Spirit. However, several scholars attest that it could possibly be a reference to Jibrīl (*peace be upon him*) as well. In other words, when a person defends the Prophet (*peace be upon him*), it is not only an angel, but the angel Jibrīl (*peace be upon him*) who is selected to guard them as was the case with Hassan ibn Thabit (*Allah's mercy be upon him*). This is the possible reward that may be awaiting you when you defend the Messenger of Allah (*peace be upon him*) using your intellect, your emotional intelligence and your patience, thereby demonstrating the true character of the Prophet (*peace be upon him*) in the process of defending him.

11) Āmīn and for You As Well

To defend your brother or sister in their absence is one thing, but to pray for them behind their back is another. When something causes you to remember someone, one of the best things that you can do is to make *du'ā'* for them. Regarding those of us who remember to mention our brother or sister when we are alone with Allah (*glorified and exalted is He*), the Prophet (*peace be upon him*) said, 'No one does that, except Allah (*glorified and exalted is He*) sends an angel'. There is a specific angel that is entrusted with praying for us (*muwakkal*) as we supplicate for another and their prayer is accepted (*mustajāb*). In one narration, the Prophet (*peace be upon him*) said, 'It is an accepted *du'ā'* and the angel will say each time آمين وَلَكَ بِمِثْلِهِ, '*āmīn*',

There is a specific angel who is entrusted with praying for us as we supplicate for another and their prayer for us is accepted.

for you as well, and so the *du'ā'* will be accepted for you and for your brother because the angel is the one that is making it'.

Subḥān Allāh! You have to ask yourself, 'Who do I feel more confident in having a *du'ā'* accepted from? Myself? Or an angel that has been specifically sent by Allah (*glorified and exalted is He*)?' This fosters a sense of selflessness where we are encouraged to engage in a prolonged fashion of making *du'ā'* for others, reassured in the knowledge that an angel whose prayer is readily accepted will be saying *'āmīn'* for us as well.

Praying for others is also one of the best ways to ward off envy. When you see something that someone has you immediately say, اللَّهُمَّ بَارِكْ لَهَا، اللَّهُمَّ بَارِكْ لَهُ, 'O Allah, bless them with that thing'. In this way, you accustom yourself to supplicating for them and it becomes a good habit. If you see something good that they have say, 'May Allah (*glorified and exalted is He*) increase it for them' and if you see them experiencing hardship say, 'May Allah (*glorified and exalted is He*) make it easy for them'. As a result, you acclimatise yourself to being able to respond to the mention of the person's name with a *du'ā'* from the heart.

Diversifying the nature of the supplications that we make for others, based upon their actual needs is something we should strive for. This can be in a generic way as mentioned in the previous paragraph or it can be more specific. For example, if someone has a medical problem, make *du'ā'* for their health, if they are in need of sustenance, ask Allah (*glorified and exalted is He*) to sustain them or if they have an issue with relatives, pray for their family. By covering all the different facets of *du'ā'* for several people, at the same time, you are also covering these aspects of your life because when you are praying for health, wealth and family, the angel is saying, *'āmīn'* for you as well. That is then written on your record, increasing your sincerity and your station with Allah (*glorified and exalted is He*).

Another thing we should strive for, when making *du'ā'* for our brothers and sisters is to do it in secret, or as the Prophet (*peace be upon him*) put it, بِظَهْرِ الْغَيْبِ, behind their back. You may mention it to the person as a means of showing solidarity with them, but not in order to boast or make them feel indebted to you (*mann*). Much in the same way as the secrecy you should try and maintain when giving charity (*ṣadaqah*), you should not

When you are praying for someone's health, wealth and family, an angel is saying 'āmīn' for you as well.

use the knowledge of your supplications to dominate someone and chip away at their self-esteem.

Imam Ahmad (*Allah's mercy be upon him*) had a list of people that he would pray for at night and he expressed that he felt more confident in his *du'ā's* for another being accepted over those he made for himself. Therefore, it was more favourable to him to engage in prolonged periods of prayer for others, rather than for himself. When you follow his example with sincerity and humility, Allah (*glorified and exalted is He*) will not only send an angel to say *'āmīn'* for you, but He will reward your selflessness by placing blessed people in your life who will *inshā' Allāh* pray for you.

12 The Best Supplication

We think of the Prophet (*peace be upon him*) in many ways, but how often do we think of him as a brother? Not just any brother but the most blessed brother, because the Prophet (*peace be upon him*) said هُمْ إِخْوَنِي هُمْ أَحِبَابِي, 'They are my brothers, they are my beloved ones, those who believe in me without having seen me'. We pray to Allah (*glorified and exalted is He*) that we are of those people who make the Messenger of Allah (*peace be upon him*) their most noble brother in faith. Therefore, if supplicating on behalf of our brothers and sisters is rewarded with the prayers of the angels, what must be the reward for sending prayers upon the Prophet (*peace be upon him*) in the form of *Ṣalawāt*?

There is a famous *ḥadīth* narrated by Ubayy ibn Ka'b (*Allah's mercy be upon him*) in which he asked the Prophet (*peace be upon him*): 'How much of my *du'ā'* should I dedicate towards sending prayers and peace upon you? I already do a great deal of it, but how much should I do?' The Prophet (*peace be upon him*) replied, 'Do as much as you wish and it will be blessed'. Ubayy ibn Ka'b (*Allah's mercy be upon him*) suggested, 'One fourth', and the Prophet (*peace be upon him*) said, 'That's good. Do more if you want and it will be blessed'. He responded, 'How about one half, O Messenger of Allah?' to which the Prophet (*peace be upon him*) replied, 'That is good and if you do more, you will be blessed'. He then suggested two-thirds and the Prophet (*peace be upon him*) said, 'That is good and if you do more you will be blessed'. Then he said, 'O Messenger of Allah! What if I dedicate the entirety of my *du'ā'* to sending prayers and peace upon you?' To this the Prophet (*peace be upon him*) said, 'If you do that, then Allah (*glorified and exalted is He*) will take care of all your concerns and forgive all of your sins'.

The meaning of this *ḥadīth* is not that we should replace our own prayers entirely with *Ṣalawāt*, as the

Prophet (*peace be upon him*) supplicated for himself
and taught his companions (*Allah's mercy be upon them*)
to do the same. Rather, it serves to highlight the
extraordinary blessings that are bestowed upon those
who pray for their most noble brother, the Messenger
of Allah (*peace be upon him*).

Ibn Taymiyyah interpreted this narration in a very
interesting way. He said that Ubayy ibn Kaʿb (*Allah's
mercy be upon him*) had a very specific *duʿā'* that he
used to make for himself at an allotted time and that
the Prophet (*peace be upon him*) was telling him that if
he replaced that *duʿā'* with *Ṣalawāt* it would cause his
concerns to be eradicated and his sins to be forgiven.
Ibn Taymiyyah connected this to the *ḥadīth* about an
angel saying *'āmīn'* for us when we supplicate on behalf
of our brother or sister in their absence, asking us to
consider that if Allah (*glorified and exalted is He*) sends
an angel when we pray for any one of our brethren,
how will He respond when we do the same for His
Messenger (*peace be upon him*)?

We can look to a whole plethora of *aḥādīth* for the
answer. They recount how, when the Prophet (*peace

be upon him) was asked why he came forth with such joy on his face he answered, 'Jibrīl came to me and said, "Does it not make you happy that no person sends *Ṣalawāt* upon you, except that Allah (*glorified and exalted is He*) sends ten times the peace and blessings upon them"'. In addition, إِلَّا صَلَّيْتُ عَلَيْهِ عَشْرًا, Jibrīl responds to each one of us as well with *Ṣalāh* and *Salām* and Allah (*glorified and exalted is He*) grants us ten good deeds, forgives ten of our sins and raises us by ten stations (*darajāt*). Other *aḥādīth* tell of how, there are angels that roam the earth looking for people that send their prayers upon the Prophet (*peace be upon him*) and convey those prayers to him. In fact, there is a specific angel that informs the Prophet (*peace be upon him*) each time someone sends *Ṣalawāt* upon him, and the Prophet (*peace be upon him*) responds by name to that *Salām* each time it is made.

The Prophet (*peace be upon him*) said, 'You can send them from any part of the earth, and the angel will convey it to me and I will respond'. That means that whether we are close to Madīnah or Makkah or not, Allah (*glorified and exalted is He*) and the angels, with Jibrīl at their helm, will all respond with prayer and blessings upon us, increasing our good deeds, removing our sins, and increasing our stations in Heaven. May Allah (*glorified and exalted is He*) increase those stations until we reach the station in the presence of the Prophet (*peace be upon him*).

*T*here is a specific angel that informs the Prophet ﷺ each time someone sends Ṣalawāt upon him, and the Prophet ﷺ responds by name to that Salām each time it is made.

Be Fair When You Judge

13

One of the assumptions that we sometimes make when we are navigating through *aḥādīth*, especially as they pertain to a crisis or dilemma, is that we are going to be at the centre of events. However, there are times when all of us will be called to judge in a dispute and one of the greatest verses on justice in the Qur'an is where Allah (*glorified and exalted is He*) says: وَلَا يَجْرِمَنَّكُمْ شَنَآنُ قَوْمٍ عَلَى أَلَّا تَعْدِلُوا That you don't let your hatred for people cause you to swerve from the path of justice. That is a quality that you rarely find, even amongst righteous people. Human beings will naturally have a bias towards those that they love or feel an affinity towards. We assume that our friends are always misunderstood even when they are wrong and our enemies are always devious even when they are right, so we end up feeling torn.

The Prophet (*peace be upon him*) talked about the difference between the formal position of a judge such as a magistrate and a person who is asked to arbitrate during a dispute, saying, 'Whoever forces themself into a position of judgment, (meaning a position of authority) will be entrusted to it'. In other words, they will not receive any blessing for it. However, regarding a person who is asked to judge and they judge righteously, the Prophet (*peace be upon him*) said, 'No person is asked to judge and they are reluctant to do so because they fear doing wrong by someone, except that Allah (*glorified and exalted is He*) sends an angel and guides them to the truth'.

'Umar ibn al-Khaṭṭāb (*Allah's mercy be upon him*) was known for the way he held everyone to the standard of justice but at the same time, showed great mercy, a combination which served to cultivate a beautiful society. He upheld that justice even when arbitrating between Muslims and non-Muslims. Sa'īd ibn al-Musayyib narrates that a Muslim and a Jew had a dispute which

No person judges in accordance with the truth, except that Allah sends two angels, one on their right and one on their left, to support them in that.

they referred to the authority of 'Umar ibn al-Khaṭṭāb (*Allah's mercy be upon him*) who judged in favour of the Jewish man over the Muslim. Upon receiving the judgement, the Jewish man said, 'You have judged correctly'. 'Umar ibn al-Khaṭṭāb (*Allah's mercy be upon him*) asked the man, وَمَا يُدْرِيكَ, 'How do you know that I judged correctly?' and he replied, 'No person judges in accordance with the truth, except that Allah (*glorified and exalted is He*) sends two angels, one on their right and one on their left, to support them in that. Once they leave the path of truth, the angels leave them'. That is something that 'Umar (*Allah's mercy be upon him*) confirmed and it is confirmed through the words of our Messenger (*peace be upon him*).

Therefore, when you are called to a dispute to judge between two people, you have a choice. You can either play the role of the Devil and perpetuate the problem by being unjust, thereby driving away the angels at your side, or you can adhere to the truth and ensure that you establish justice to the best of your ability and Allah (*glorified and exalted is He*) will send a special angel to assist you in doing so.

The Seeker of Knowledge

14

There is nothing more blessed than when you are leaving home with the banner of the angels over your head, angels in front and behind you and an angel above you who is using their reins to elevate your station with Allah (*glorified and exalted is He*). What is going to determine the actions of those angels is the intention that you have as you go out into the world. To leave your home with the intention of seeking or spreading knowledge that brings you closer to the Creator (*glorified and exalted is He*) is the most noble pursuit that we find in the Sunnah of the Prophet (*peace be upon him*).

The Messenger of Allah (*peace be upon him*) said, 'Whoever seeks out a path of knowledge, Allah (*glorified and exalted is He*) will make the path of Paradise easy for them' and 'No one leaves their house seeking knowledge except that the angels lower their wings in approval for that person'. One of the most famous *aḥādīth*, upon which Ibn Rajab based an entire book, states that, as a person pursues knowledge, the inhabitants of both the Heavens and the earth all seek forgiveness for that person. Whether it is the angels above or the fish in the sea, each one of them seeks forgiveness for that person as they go out seeking and spreading knowledge. The Prophet (*peace be upon him*) also said, 'The superiority of the learned man over the devout worshipper is like that of the full moon over the stars', and in another narration, 'The likeness of a scholar to a worshipper is akin to my rank over the lowest of you'. This is because the one who seeks and spreads knowledge, spreads good in the same way that the angels spread their wings.

In the same narration, the Prophet (*peace be upon him*) said, 'The learned are the heirs of the Prophets (*Allah's mercy be upon them*) who bequeath neither dinar nor dirham, but only knowledge'. In other words, knowledge is the inheritance of the Prophets (*Allah's mercy be upon them*). Therefore, the pursuit of knowledge serves as a means of bringing us closer to Allah (*glorified and exalted is He*) as we learn about Him and His Creation. Knowledge becomes a means of connecting us to the Prophet (*peace be upon him*) because we become an inheritor of the Prophet (*peace be upon him*) and a means of connecting us to the angels because they spread their wings in approval of our actions. Finally, it serves as a positive connection with our fellow brothers and sisters because our relationship with them is benefitting them.

Another very important point that Ibn Rajab makes is that by seeking knowledge of Allah (*glorified and exalted is He*) we even begin to revere the environment in a new way. In their understanding of the earth as Allah's creation, the scholar considers the rights of all creatures inhabiting it and strives to protect those rights. Why else would even the fishes seek forgiveness for that person?

The example of a person who spreads and seeks knowledge in comparison with the one who worships Allah (*glorified and exalted is He*) is like someone who earns Halal, which is good and someone who, spends in the cause of Allah (*glorified and exalted is He*) which contains immense reward.

For the Muslim who is able to dedicate years of study to the sacred knowledge, there is indeed great reward in store. However, just by making the effort to pursue even one line of knowledge, we can all share in the blessings. Instead of accessing knowledge online, why not make the physical effort to go out and seek that knowledge? In doing so, you too can enjoy the blessing of having the angels lower their wings for you and all of Allah's creation seeking forgiveness for you.

15 No Strings Attached

'I love you for the sake of Allah (*glorified and exalted is He*)'. What exactly does that statement mean? When someone tells you they love you for the sake of Allah (*glorified and exalted is He*) or when you say it to someone else, are you suggesting that you *only* love them for the sake of Allah (*glorified and exalted is He*)? What if you also love them for something else?

According to the scholars, when you say to someone, أُحِبُّكَ فِي اللهِ, I love you for the sake of Allah (*glorified and exalted is He*), which is what the Prophet (*peace be upon him*) told his companion, Muʿādh (*Allah's mercy be upon him*) it means that you love them solely for that reason, with no other motive attached. The response

When you say to someone, 'I love you for the sake of Allah', which is what the Prophet ﷺ told Muʿādh ﵁, it means that you love them solely for that reason, with no other motive attached.

to that, أَحَبَّكَ اللهُ الَّذِي أَحْبَبْتَنِي فِيهِ, may the One who you love me for, love you back, demonstrates that the greatest reward that could come from uttering those words is not a confirmation of the other person's love, but that Allah (*glorified and exalted is He*) responds to your love with His love.

The Prophet (*peace be upon him*) gave the example of a man who went out to visit a brother of his for the sake of Allah (*glorified and exalted is He*). An angel came to him in the form of a human being and asked him, 'Where are you going?' The man replied, 'I'm going to visit my brother for the sake of Allah (*glorified and exalted is He*)'. The angel then asked, 'Is there anything that you want from him? Does he owe you anything?' to which the man replied, 'No'. The angel asked, 'Are you trying to get some favour out of him?' and the man said, 'No'. The angel asked, 'Is he a powerful man? Or does he owe you something? Is this to gently remind him about something else so that the next time you plan to visit him he will remember?' The man responded, لَا، غَيْرَ أَنِّي أَحْبَبْتُهُ فِي اللهِ, 'The only reason I am going to visit him is because I love him for the sake of Allah (*glorified and exalted is He*)'. The angel then told him, فَإِنِّي رَسُولُ اللهِ إِلَيْكَ, 'I am a messenger of Allah (*glorified and exalted is He*) and I have been sent to tell you that Allah (*glorified and exalted is He*) loves you just as you love your brother for Him'.

This narration should prompt us all to ask ourselves, 'When is the last time I visited someone purely for the sake of Allah (*glorified and exalted is He*)?' That does not mean you do not love a person for the sake of Allah (*glorified and exalted is He*) but it may be that when calling or visiting them, you have an ulterior motive. You realise you want something or that the person is in a position to benefit your worldly affairs and that is a motivating factor for you, but when is the last time you came together with someone purely for the sake of Allah (*glorified and exalted is He*)?

In another narration, the Prophet (*peace be upon him*) said, 'Whoever visits the sick, or his brother for the sake of Allah (*glorified and exalted is He*), an angel calls out, نَادَى مُنَادٍ؛ طِبْتَ وَطَابَ مَمْشَاكَ وَتَبَوَّأْتَ مِنَ الجَنَّةِ مَنْزِلًا. *Ṭibta*, meaning, 'May you be purified and find goodness in your path always', is a very comprehensive way of praying for that person. The angels follow with

Whoever visits the sick, or his brother for the sake of Allah, an angel calls out, 'May you be purified and find goodness in your path always, may your steps be blessed and may you have a special station in Paradise.'

طِبْتَ وَطَابَ مَمْشَاكَ and 'may your steps be blessed' which is a reference to everything that you walk towards in your worldly affairs. Finally, وَتَبَوَّأْتَ مِنَ الجَنَّةِ مَنْزِلًا, 'may you have a special station in Paradise, an abode close to Allah (*glorified and exalted is He*)'.

The angel's supplication encompasses everything we could want in this world and the next. Therefore, there is no need to visit someone with the intention of procuring any of these things. Just by going for the sake of Allah (*glorified and exalted is He*) and to establish that relationship with Allah (*glorified and exalted is He*), we are rewarded with all the things that only our Lord (*glorified and exalted is He*) can provide.

The Ultimate Healer

We previously established the rewards in store for the one who visits their sick brother or sister for the sake of Allah (*glorified and exalted is He*), but what does Allah (*glorified and exalted is He*) say about the one who is sick? The one who is inflicted with illness or fever and is suffering at home or in a hospital. What is their status with their Lord (*glorified and exalted is He*) and what role do the angels play in accompanying that person as they are in that situation?

The Prophet (*peace be upon him*) said, 'When a person is ill, Allah (*glorified and exalted is He*) sends two angels to accompany that person in their illness'. Not only do those two angels record the reward for the sick person's

visitors, they also monitor their response to those
visitors. That means that if you are unwell and someone
asks how you are, you have two choices. You may
choose to complain and talk about how bad you feel or
you may say, اَلْحَمْدُ لِله, *Alḥamdulillāh*, praise be to Allah
(*glorified and exalted is He*) for what I still have. If you
describe your situation, it is only for the sake of giving
an accurate picture of what you are experiencing and to
reiterate, اَلْحَمْدُ لِله, all praise and thanks are due to Allah
(*glorified and exalted is He*) for what He has spared me
in the midst of this sickness.

Whichever response you choose will be recorded by the
angels and reported to Allah (*glorified and exalted is He*).
The Prophet (*peace be upon him*) said, 'They look at what
he says to his visitors. If he praises Allah (*glorified and
exalted is He*) and lauds Him when they come to him,
they take that up to Allah (*glorified and exalted is He*)'
and Allah (*glorified and exalted is He*) responds with
these words:

*If I cause my slave to die as a result of this illness, then I
will surely grant that person a garden in Jannah. Should
I heal my slave, then I will replace their flesh with better*

*flesh and their blood with better blood and I will efface
their evil actions.*

Allah (*glorified and exalted is He*) is saying, 'I will give
that person لَحْمًا خَيْرًا مِنْ لَحْمِهِ, flesh that is better than
the flesh they already have, دَمًا خَيْرًا مِنْ دَمِهِ, blood that
is better than the blood they already have and I will
wipe out their sins' and if your Lord (*glorified and
exalted is He*) causes you to die, then you will have
Jannah assured because of the way that you responded
to your suffering.

Generally speaking, if you show patience in the face of
hardship, that patience will be rewarded, but the sick
person enjoys a privileged status with Allah (*glorified
and exalted is He*) which explains why there is such
reward in visiting the sick as well as for the sick person
who still praises Allah (*glorified and exalted is He*). This
is evidenced in the following narration:

The Prophet (*peace be upon him*) said, 'On the Day of
Judgment, when a person stands before Allah (*glorified
and exalted is He*), they will be asked, "O My servant,
O son of Adam, I was hungry and you did not feed Me".

When a person is ill, Allah sends two angels to accompany them in their illness. The angels record the reward for the sick person's visitors and also monitor their response to those visitors.

And the person will reply, "O my Lord, how can I feed You. You are the Lord of the worlds?" and Allah (*glorified and exalted is He*) will respond, "Do you not know that My servant was hungry and had you gone to my servant and fed him, لَوَجَدْتَ ذَلِكَ عِندِي، يَا ابْنَ آدَمَ, then you would have found that reward with Me, or with that person". Then Allah (*glorified and exalted is He*) will say, "O My servant, I was thirsty and you did not nourish Me," and the person will reply, "O Allah! How can I nourish You? You are the Lord of the worlds!" and Allah (*glorified and exalted is He*) will respond once again, "Don't you know that My servant was thirsty and had you given them something to nourish themselves with, لَوَجَدْتَ ذَلِكَ عِندِي، يَا ابْنَ آدَمَ, you would have found that reward with Me". Then Allah (*glorified and exalted is He*) says, "O son of Adam, I was sick and you did not visit Me" and that person will reply, "How could I visit You and You are the Lord of the worlds?" and Allah (*glorified and exalted is He*) will say, "Do you not know My servant was sick, and had you gone to him لَوْ عُدْتَهُ لَوَجَدْتَنِي عِنْدَهُ، يَا ابْنَ آدَمَ, you would have found Me with him'".

The last reply is highly significant, 'You would have found Me, O son of Adam, not My reward'. In other words, when you are sick and respond to your illness with patience, it is not just the reward of Allah (*glorified and exalted is He*) that is with you, but Allah (*glorified and exalted is He*) Himself that is by your side.

An Entourage of 17 of 70,000

The Prophet (*peace be upon him*) said, 'When someone goes to visit their brother or sister who is ill, for the sake of Allah (*glorified and exalted is He*), 70,000 angels accompany them on that visit, all praying and seeking forgiveness for that person throughout the entire day, through to the next morning'. Consider how incredible that is. A 70,000 strong entourage of angels that are far greater than human beings, all praying and seeking forgiveness for you, solely because you took the time to visit someone who is sick for the sake of your Lord (*glorified and exalted is He*).

There are many people in this day and age that give charity for the sake of Allah (*glorified and exalted is*

He), perform voluntary fasts, pray *Qiyām al-Layl* and undertake other initiatives such as feeding the poor, but how rare it is to find those that visit sick people purely for the sake of Allah (*glorified and exalted is He*). This does not mean someone who has been called to do so in a pastoral capacity such as a Chaplain at a hospital or that person's family members, but applies only to those individuals or groups who make visiting the sick a religious duty and a way of connecting with their Lord (*glorified and exalted is He*).

The Prophet (*peace be upon him*) tells us that the Muslim who visits a sick person for the sake of Allah (*glorified and exalted is He*) will be in the company of 70,000 angels, but what is the significance of the number 70,000? During his Night Journey *(al-Isrā' Wa'l-Miʿrāj)*, the Prophet (*peace be upon him*) witnessed the 70,000 angels that daily visit the heavenly House of Allah (*Al bait al Maʿmūr*) which is right above the Kaʿbah. The angels make their Ṭawāf and then 70,000 of them enter the Kaʿbah and never return. Some scholars connect this with the reward for visiting the sick as the sick person has such a unique position with Allah (*glorified and exalted is He*) that it is like Allah (*glorified and exalted is He*) is there with them during their hardship. This re-enforces the message of the *ḥadīth* that was discussed previously in which Allah (*glorified and exalted is He*) tells His servant that it is not His reward, but He, Himself that can be found beside the sick person.

In addition to an entourage of angels to accompany them, the Prophet (*peace be upon him*) said of the person who visits their sick brother or sister, وَكَانَ لَهُ خَرِيْفٌ فِي الجَنَّةِ, and then that person will have a special garden for them promised in Paradise. We previously established that Allah (*glorified and exalted is He*) has promised the person who is ill that if they pass away as a result of their illness, they will be granted a garden in Jannah. Therefore, just as when you pray for your brother or sister, and the angel says آمِين وَلَكَ بِمِثْلِهِ, *āmīn*, and for you as well, when you visit your brother or sister who is gravely ill, you too will receive the reward of a garden in Heaven as they have been promised. As for visiting the person who is ill, serious or otherwise, you are assured that just as the angels will be praying for them, a 70,000 strong entourage will be praying for you.

When someone goes to visit their brother or sister who is ill, for the sake of Allah, 70,000 angels accompany them on that visit, all praying and seeking forgiveness for that person throughout the entire day until the next morning.

When Your Loved Ones Are Dying

18

Being around someone who is dying is the most potent reminder of the true value of life. It is something many of us are now deprived of as people who are dying are more often left in the hands of professionals like medical staff, but seeing someone take their last breath and knowing that مَلَكُ المَوْتِ, the Angel of Death has just entered the room is a truly humbling experience. You witness the moment where their eyes become fixed in one direction and then the soul leaves the body. The Prophet (*peace be upon him*) described how when some people are leaving this world, they have the angels of mercy coming towards them whereas others look like something horrifying is approaching them. Only Allah (*glorified and exalted is He*) knows what is actually happening, but anyone who has been around dying people on a frequent basis attest to the difference in how people leave this world at those moments.

The Prophet (*peace be upon him*) said, 'Verily, when the soul leaves the body, the eyes follow the soul, 'إِذَا قُبِضَ الرُّوحُ تَبِعَهُ البَصَرُ' and his Sunnah was to then close the eyelids of that person which he did with many of his Companions including Abū Salamah (*Allah's mercy be upon him*). Umm Salamah (*Allah's mercy be upon her*) recounts, 'When the Prophet (*peace be upon him*) entered in and Abū Salamah (*Allah's mercy be upon him*) was taking his dying breaths, his eyes became fixed and then he passed. As the Prophet (*peace be upon him*) was closing his eyelids, the people started to wail and weep and the Prophet (*peace be upon him*) told them, "Do not supplicate for anything but good, for the angels say '*āmīn*' to what you say"'.

Subḥān Allāh! The angels will say, '*āmīn*', so as you are praying for the deceased in those moments, make sure your words will be of benefit to them because the angels who have just entered the room to reclaim their soul will be responding with '*āmīn*'. The examples of

As you are praying for someone in their last moments, make sure your words will be of benefit to them because the angels who have just entered the room to reclaim their soul will be responding with 'āmīn'.

the supplications we should be offering can be found
in the same narration where the Prophet (*peace be upon
him*) said, اللَّهُمَّ اغْفِرْ لِأَبِي سَلَمَةَ, O Allah! Forgive Abū
Salamah, وَارْفَعْ دَرَجَتَهُ فِي الْمَهْدِيِّينَ, and raise his station,
make his station high amongst Your rightly guided
servants, وَافْسَحْ لَهُ فِي قَبْرِهِ, and expand his grave,
وَنَوِّرْ لَهُ فِيهِ, and put light in his expansive grave,
وَاخْلُفْهُ فِي عَقِبِهِ, and take of the descendants whom he's
left behind, to make them pious, and take care of them.

Imagine, then, how important your prayers are in
those moments when the angels are present to reclaim
the soul of your friend or loved one. The prayers you
offer in their final moments and just after, will either
work for, or against them as their soul is taken, either
to a high place in Paradise or to a place (*May Allah,
glorified and exalted is He, protect us*) that is worse than
that which they encountered in this world.

An Angel in Human Form

19

Have you ever come across a person in your life that you thought might be an angel? Someone who just emerged in your hour of need or someone who you helped who then disappeared as suddenly as they had appeared in your life and you thought to yourself, 'This person can't be a human being'. Could it be that the person was really an angel in human form?

There is a *ḥadīth* in which the Prophet (*peace be upon him*) talks about three men from Banī Isrā'īl and they were contemporaries as is made clear in the *ḥadīth*. One of them was bald, the other a leper and the third man was blind. One day an angel approached all three of them and asked, 'What is it that you want to change about yourself?' The leper replied, 'I want to have good skin because the people feel an aversion towards me because of my leprosy'. The angel touched him and he was cured. Then the angel asked the man, 'What type of property is most beloved to you?' and the man replied, 'camels' and so the angel presented him with a pregnant she-camel, saying, بَارَكَ اللهُ لَكَ فِيهَا May Allah (*glorified and exalted is He*) bless you with this she-camel'. This shows that it is Allah (*glorified and exalted is He*) that is going to provide, not the angel and the valley of camels that was then borne out of the she-camel is a testament to Allah's generosity.

When the angel asked the bald man what he would like to change about himself, he replied, 'A good head of hair that will beautify me' and so the angel touched the man's head and hair grew where there was none. The angel then asked him, 'What type of property is most beloved to you?' and the man replied, 'cows'. The angel presented him with a pregnant cow, saying, بَارَكَ اللهُ لَكَ فِيهَا, May Allah (*glorified and exalted is He*) bless you with it and suddenly he had an entire herd of cows. Finally, the angel asked the same question to the blind man and the blind man replied, 'I would love to have my eyesight back' and so the angel wiped his hands over the man's eyes and restored his vision. The angel then asked him, 'What is the most beloved of property to you?' and the blind man replied, 'sheep', so the angel gifted him with a pregnant ewe who gave birth to a whole flock of sheep.

In the future, the angel returns to all three of the men in different human forms. To the leper, the angel shows himself as a poor man with leprosy, to the one who was bald, the angel shows up as a poor man with no hair and to the one whose sight he restored, he shows himself as a poor man who is blind. He asks each of the men for support, but the leper and the bald man deny that they were ever poor and turn him away. The angel gives them the opportunity to redeem themselves, asking each of them in turn, 'Were you not once in need yourself?' but both have forgotten the blessings of Allah (*glorified and exalted is He*) and their arrogance causes them to once again deny their past. The angel then says, 'If you are lying, then may Allah (*glorified and exalted is He*) return you to what you were before'. Now, there are multiple rewards that

you find in the *aḥādīth* for the person that is blind
and patient with Allah (*glorified and exalted is He*),
and in this narration also, the blind man passes
the angel's teſt. As soon as he sees the angel in the
guise of what was once his own form, he tells him,
'Take from this property whatever you want for I was
once like you and Allah (*glorified and exalted is He*)
provided for me'.

As the scholars point out, it was the laſt of the three
men who was in the worſt situation and yet he is the
moſt humble, showing kindness to his brother and
gratitude to his Lord (*glorified and exalted is He*) without
even being prompted to do so. His humility is rewarded
when the angel says to him, 'Keep your property with
you, فَقَدْ رَضِيَ اللهُ عِنْكَ وَسَخِطَ عَلَى صَاحِبِكَ because verily
Allah (*glorified and exalted is He*) is pleased with you
and angry with your two companions'. As a result, the
two companions lose everything they have and are
reſtored back to their former positions and the blind
man is not only able to keep the worldly blessings Allah
(*glorified and exalted is He*) has beſtowed upon him but
is also increased in his ſtation in the hereafter.

The moral of the story is to honour your brother and sister in need because you never really know who you are encountering. When you ask yourself, 'Did I just come across an angel?' remember that only Allah (*glorified and exalted is He*) knows the answer. An angel will not reveal themselves because that would defeat the purpose of the test. Therefore, we should strive to treat each and every person we meet with kindness, humility and dignity, remembering always our own vulnerability and the blessings that have been bestowed upon us as we never really know who our Lord (*glorified and exalted is He*) has placed in front of us.

We should strive to treat each and every person we meet with kindness, humility and dignity, remembering always our own vulnerability and the blessings that have been bestowed upon us, as we never really know who our Lord has placed in front of us.

A Caller From Heaven's Gates

20

The Prophet (*peace be upon him*) said, 'When a person wakes up each morning, two angels are sent to him. One angel says, اللَّهُمَّ أَعْطِ مُنْفِقًا خَلَفًا and the other one says, اللَّهُمَّ أَعْطِ مُمْسِكًا تَلَفًا, O Allah give to the one who spends in charity (*ṣadaqah*), and withhold from the one who withholds charity'. When discussing this *ḥadīth*, Imam Siraj said that it is not just the people in front of you who are documenting on paper or on spreadsheets, the amounts you give in *ṣadaqah*, but that there is a book in which the angels are recording those amounts. The Imam then asked, 'When your name is there, do you want there to be a zero next to your name or do you want there to be something else?' In other words, we should never allow there to be a zero next to our name when it comes to giving charity.

In another *ḥadīth* from Ibn Ḥibbān, we are provided with a beautiful illustration of the first narration. The Prophet (*peace be upon him*) said, 'Verily, there is an angel at one of the gates of Paradise that is holding on to that gate and saying, مَن يُقرِضُ اليَومَ يُجزْى غَدًا, "Whoever gives a beautiful loan today will be given a beautiful reward tomorrow" and at another gate of Paradise, there is another angel saying, اللَّهُمَّ أَعْطِ مُنْفِقًا خَلَفًا، اللَّهُمَّ أَعْطِ مُمْسِكًا تَلَفًا, "O Allah, give to the one who gives, and withhold from the one who withholds"'.

Another *ḥadīth* tells the story of a man who heard a voice from the clouds as he was walking one day. The voice said, اسْقِ حَدِيقَةَ فُلَانٍ, 'Irrigate the garden of so-and-so, water the garden of so-and-so,' and as the man looked up, he saw the clouds form and suddenly it began to pour with rain. He watched as the rain formed into a perfect channel and flowed directly into this garden. The owner of the garden was then distributing the water across his land and the man

asked him what his story was without telling him
what he had just seen. The other man was hesitant,
but curious as to why he was being asked and then
the man told him, 'I saw the clouds form and I heard
a voice from the sky that said, "Water the garden of
so-and-so" and that is why I came to you'. Upon hearing
this, the owner of the garden told him, 'Everything that
I earn, I divide into three. One-third is for my family,
one-third that I invest, and one-third that I give in
charity. That is how I allocate all of my wealth'. This is
a divine equation for good in our lives and shows that
charity should be a daily habit, rather than something
we indulge in during big fundraisers or only at certain
times of the year. Do not wait for someone else to
invite you to Paradise. This is your reward to claim and
something that is between you and Allah (*glorified and
exalted is He*).

Let me share something personal with you. One of
the things that my parents did (*May Allah have mercy
on my mother and preserve my father*), we used to have
for one of the charities we used to give to, قُبَّةُ الصَّخْرَة,
the dome of the rock. This was a money box and the
dome would come off and we would put some charity

in there, every single day. And so, whether it's a dollar that was put in, or a coin a day, it was just to get us in the habit of everyone putting in something, a penny, a nickel, something every single day that goes towards *ṣadaqah* and then at the end of the month, we'd give it away in charity.

Giving charity is a daily habit we should teach our families as well even if it is just placing a bottle or money box in the house where everyone can add some loose change each day. In doing so, we are inviting the opportunity for an angel, literally holding on to the gates of Paradise, to pray for us and our loved ones to be rewarded with a place therein.

21 | *The First Rows*

One of the things that causes a person to be shaded by the Throne of Allah (*glorified and exalted is He*) is their love for the mosque. In the narration of Abū Saʿīd (*Allah's mercy be upon him*), the Prophet (*peace be upon him*) said, 'If you see a person consistent with the mosque, فَاشْهَدُوا لَهُ بِالإِيمَانِ, then bear witness that that is a person with faith'. Although it is not one of the stronger *aḥādīth*, the meaning is correct, and it is usually the people that are most committed to the mosque that we see in the front row. At many of the mosques we attend, this is often the elders, that we can be guilty of mocking for always being the first to arrive and ensure themselves a front row place. However, rather than denigrating them, we should be humbled by the example they are

The Prophet ﷺ said, 'Allah and His angels send their blessings upon the first row.' Just as you have people who are very punctual with the things that are important to them, there are those who possess the mindset of always being in the front row.

setting as the Prophet (*peace be upon him*) said, أَصْحَابُ الصَّفِ الأَوَّلِ؛ إِنَّ الله وَمَلَائِكَتَهُ يُصَلُّونَ عَلَى الصَّفِ الأُوَلِ 'Allah (*glorified and exalted is He*) and His angels send their blessings upon the first row'.

Of course, the significance of being in the first row goes beyond the physical. It is about the way that person has adjusted themselves and their mindset in order to be there before the Imam says, اَللَّهُ أَكْبَر, '*Allahu Akbar*' and just as you have people that are very punctual with the things that are important to them, there are those who possess the mindset of always being in the front row. It is usually the same people we see each time we attend the mosque and those are the people being recognised and blessed by the angels for their dedication to Allah (*glorified and exalted is He*).

When you read the books of the pious predecessors (*the Salaf*), one of the descriptions used for someone who repented and changed their life was that they became from the, أَصْحَابُ الصَّفِ الأَوَّلِ, the people that were always in the first row. That was one of the ways in which they recognised that a person's repentance was sincere and that they really had turned back to Allah (*glorified and exalted is He*) and they were of those who attended the mosque, seeking purification, يَتَطَهَّرُوا, as attested by Allah (*glorified and exalted is He*).

The Prophet (*peace be upon him*) said that one of the blessings of this *Ummah* is that Allah (*glorified and exalted is He*) has established our prayer in the same way that the angels line up for their prayer. Therefore, the way that we form our rows is identical to the way in which the angels form their rows before Allah (*glorified and exalted is He*). When the angels witness those people that are coming early to the mosque and lining up in the same way that they line up before their Lord (*glorified and exalted is He*) it causes them to rejoice and their joy is evidenced in the supplications they make for us.

In another *ḥadīth*, the Prophet (*peace be upon him*) said, 'Allah (*glorified and exalted is He*) and His angels send blessings upon the right side of the row'. This is in reference to when the congregational row is imbalanced. The Imam should be centred as much

One of the blessings of this Ummah is that Allah has established our prayer in the same way that the angels line up for their prayer.

as possible, but if there is an imbalance, it should be to the right. This is because the angels always fill the right side of the row before the left, reiterating the connection between ourselves and the angels during *Ṣalāh*. It is the same connection that is established by those in the front row who have arrived on time to worship, longing and anticipating communion with their Lord (*glorified and exalted is He*), just as the angels do. It is no wonder, then that those people are recognised and elevated by Allah (*glorified and exalted is He*) and His heavenly congregation.

The Friday Roll Book

There are two things that will cause you to rush to get somewhere as quickly as possible. Either it is who you want to see or what is being given out and those are the two things that are spoken about when Allah (*glorified and exalted is He*) talks about the Friday Prayer (*Ṣalāt al-Jumuʿah*).

Generally, those people who are in the first row of the congregation for *Jumuʿah* can also be found in the front row for Fajr and ʿIsha' prayers each day, but for those of us who are unable to attend the other prayers, it is worth noting the profound way in which Allah (*glorified and exalted is He*) talks about the Friday prayer in particular,

يَآ أَيُّهَا الَّذِينَ أَمَنُوا اِذَا نُوْدِىَ لِلصَّلَاةِ مِنْ يَوْمِ الْجُمُعَةِ فَاسْعَوْا إِلَى ذِكْرِ اللهِ وَذَرُوا الْبَيْعَ

'When the call of *Jumuʿah* is made, rush to the remembrance of Allah and leave behind your trade'. In other words, leave behind those worldly things that distract you from your *Ṣalāh*.

On the pulpit of Kufah, ʿAlī ibn Abī Ṭālib (*Allah's mercy be upon him*) said, 'Every Friday when you wake up, the devils go to the market place with their banners'. This ties back to the *ḥadīth* which speaks of whether an angel or a devil will hold a banner above our heads each day when we leave our homes and on Friday, the devils use their banners to distract people with the things that are of this world so that they are delayed in attending *Jumuʿah*. Meanwhile, the angels occupy the entrances of the mosques from the very start of the morning right through to the *Jumuʿah* prayer. The Prophet (*peace be upon him*) said these angels document who is coming, in accordance with how early they arrive, الأَوَّلُ فَالأَوَّلُ, first by first.

The first to come on that day are those that come in
the first hour between what the scholars interpret as
sunrise (*al-shurūq*) and *Jumuʿah* and they are likened
to the one who sacrifices a camel for the sake of Allah
(*glorified and exalted is He*). Those who arrive in the
next hour are like the one who sacrifices a cow for
the sake of Allah (*glorified and exalted is He*). The
people who come in the third hour are like the one
who sacrifices a ram for the sake of Allah (*glorified
and exalted is He*) and the Prophet (*peace be upon him*)
described the continuing decrease in reward until
finally he came to the one who arrives in the last hour
of whom he said, 'they are like the one who sacrifices
a hen or an egg for the sake of Allah (*glorified and
exalted is He*)'. Then the Messenger of Allah (*peace be
upon him*) said, 'When the Imam rises to the pulpit
and says السَّلامُ عَلَيْكُم, *Assalāmu ʿalaykum,* the angels
roll up their scrolls and listen to the sermon (*khuṭbah*)'.
Subḥān Allāh! This means, if you are giving a *khuṭbah*,
angels are among your audience and if you are
listening and find yourself distracted, remember that
the angels are listening with you. It is those same
angels that were recording the chronological order of
the congregation as they arrived.

Despite the rewards on offer, there is always a rush of people missing the *khuṭbah* and arriving just before the *Ṣalāh*. The Prophet (*peace be upon him*) gave an example of how people would hasten to the mosque if there were material things being distributed and yet the people who do not hasten towards the Friday prayer are missing out on the rewards of Allah (*glorified and exalted is He*).

In a narration from 'Abdullah Ibn Masʿud (*Allah's mercy be upon him*) the Prophet (*peace be upon him*) said, 'Every Friday in Paradise, the people gather in the *Sūq*, the special place of *Jannah*, and Allah (*glorified and exalted is He*) addresses them'. So, even in Paradise Fridays are special because, for those whose station is not high enough to see their Lord (*glorified and exalted is He*) every day, they are guaranteed to see Him at least once a week. Ibn Masʿud (*Allah's mercy be upon him*) continues, 'Those that are closest to Allah (*glorified and exalted is He*) during the Friday gatherings in Paradise are those that hastened to the mosque for *Jumuʿah* prayers'.

To conclude, the closer you are to Allah (*glorified and exalted is He*) during *Jumuʿah* in Jannah is determined by how close you are to the Imam during *Jumuʿah* in this world. In other words, those who arrive early and listen attentively. That is why it is so important for us all to hasten to Friday prayers and by doing so, we express to Allah (*glorified and exalted is He*) that it is not just that we want to be included in the angel's roll book each Friday, but that we want to be recorded amongst those who strove to be as close to Him (*glorified and exalted is He*) as possible.

*T*hose who are closest to Allah during the Friday gatherings in Paradise are those who hastened to the mosque for Jumu'ah prayers.

23 From Prayer to Prayer

The main factor in determining the quality of your prayer is what you do before and after it. Just as with anything else, it begins with the preparation. There is such a difference between the person who takes time to declutter their mind and prepare themselves before prayer and someone who just rushes into it between other activities.

One of the best ways you can utilise the time before and after your prayer is by pairing it with other forms of remembrance. The Prophet (*peace be upon him*) encourages us to read *Sūrah al-Kahf* on Friday, so making it a habit before the Friday prayer means not only do you reap the reward of reading the surah on that day, but that your early arrival to the mosque will be recorded by the angels at the entrance.

Likewise, when it comes to regular prayers, the best way to maintain a daily regimen of remembrance of Allah (*glorified and exalted is He*), whether that is recitation of the Qur'an or a particular supplication, is by connecting it to your daily prayers. The added benefit is that it will keep you in your place of prayer. The Prophet (*peace be upon him*) said, 'The angels continue to pray for you so long as you remain where you pray and do not invalidate your ablution. They continue to pray for you, saying, اَللَّهُمَّ اغْفِرْلَهُ اَللَّهُمَّ ارْحَمْهُ, O Allah forgive him, O Allah have mercy on him, O Allah forgive him, O Allah have mercy on him'.

When applying this idea to the mosque, we can again look to the Sunnah of the Prophet (*peace be upon him*) who said to his Companions (*Allah's mercy be upon them*), 'Should I not tell you of deeds that cause Allah (*glorified and exalted is He*) to obliterate your sins and elevate your ranks?' and the Companions (*Allah's mercy be upon them*) replied, 'What is it O Messenger of Allah?' The Prophet (*peace be upon him*) said, 'Three things: When you perform ablution thoroughly, you increase your steps to the mosque and you stay in the mosque between two prayers'. A practical way of doing this is by connecting two prayers that have the shortest duration between them such as Maghrib and 'Ishā'. Even if you are only able to commit to it once a week or even monthly, dedicate that time to the remembrance of Allah (*glorified and exalted is He*).

The Prophet (*peace be upon him*) referred to the one who does so as, ذَلِكُمُ الرِّبَاطُ , like a person who is on guard in a battle, except that the enemy is your base-self (*nafs*), مُجَاهَدَةُ النَّفْسِ and you are striving against yourself. Therefore, it is like you are holding a station in battle when you are between Maghrib and 'Ishā', and that is a way by which Allah (*glorified and exalted is He*) obliterates your sins and elevates your ranks.

The immense reward for staying in the mosque between two prayers is further evidenced in the following narration by 'Abdullāh ibn 'Amr ibn al-'Āṣ (*Allah's mercy be upon him*):

We were sitting in the *masjid* between Maghrib and 'Ishā' and the Prophet (*peace be upon him*) came back after the *Ṣalāh*, pulling up his garment and running so fast that he was short of breath, in order to tell us something urgent. He (*peace be upon him*) asked us, 'Have you been here for this entire time between these two prayers?' to which we replied, 'yes', and the Prophet (*peace be upon him*) said to us, 'One of the gates of Heaven just opened and Allah (*glorified and exalted is He*) was praising you to the angels, يُبَاهِي بِكُمُ المَلَائَكَةَ, saying, أُنْظُرُوا إِلَى عِبَادِي, Look at my servants! قَدْ قَضَوْا فَرِيضَةً وَهُمْ يَنْتَظِرُونَ أُخْرَى, They have finished one obligatory prayer and they are waiting for the next one'.

The narration beautifully illustrates the way in which using the time between prayers in worship is an act which inspires the pleasure of Allah (*glorified and exalted is He*) and so, whenever you consider how to use the time before and after your *Ṣalāh*, think back to the examples of the Prophet (*peace be upon him*) and his Companions (*Allah's mercy be upon them*) and fill it with remembrance of Allah (*glorified and exalted is He*) in the knowledge that all the while, the angels are sending their blessings upon you.

Struggling to Recite

24

There is a well-known *ḥadīth* in which the Prophet (*peace be upon him*) describes a man who finds his camel carrying all his belongings after thinking he had lost everything and was going to die in the desert. The man is so overjoyed to find he has been delivered that when he calls out to Allah (*glorified and exalted is He*), he stumbles and says, أَنْتَ عَبْدِي وَأَنَا رَبُّكَ, You are my servant and I am your Lord. Mixing it up out of مِنْ شِدَّةِ الْفَرَحِ, because of his excitement in those moments. The Prophet (*peace be upon him*) concludes, 'Allah (*glorified and exalted is He*) is more pleased with the repentance of one of you than that man would be when he found his camel'.

This narration beautifully illustrates how Allah (*glorified and exalted is He*), far from being displeased when the man stumbles on his words, loves to see His servant in his brokenness when he turns to Him, recognising it as a sign of the man's overwhelming gratitude and humility. If Allah (*glorified and exalted is He*) derives such pleasure from someone's broken supplication, what then does he feel for the one who struggles through their Qur'an recitation?

The Prophet (*peace be upon him*) said, اَلْمَاهِرُ بِالقُرآنِ مَعَ السَّفَرَةِ الكِرَامِ البَرَرَة, ''The one who is proficient with the recitation of the Qur'an is with the كِرَامٍ بَرَرَةٍ, noble and righteous scribes from the angels and the one who recites the Qur'an and stumbles over it, وَهُوَ عَلَيهِ شَاقٌّ, struggles with it, will have two times the reward. This may be in reference to the new Muslim or just someone who is not used to recitation. They hear others recite the Qur'an beautifully, with *tajwīd* and although they do not believe they can reach such proficiency, they make the effort to learn. They learn Arabic, they recite daily and they attend Qur'an circles. They know they will struggle and stumble, but they allow their humility, not their pride to lead them in that process.

The one who is proficient with the recitation of the Qur'an is with the noble and righteous scribes from the angels and the one who recites the Qur'an and stumbles over it, struggles with it, will have two times the reward.

It is an important *ḥadīth* because it shows you that the struggle itself is worship and arrogance is a barrier and a hindrance to bettering yourself in the sight of Allah (*glorified and exalted is He*). And so, that student puts aside their ego and humbles themselves in the presence of their teacher and their peers in order to obtain the pleasure of Allah (*glorified and exalted is He*). If Allah (*glorified and exalted is He*) loves to see the humble servant who stumbles in his supplication, how blessed must be the one who struggles through the Qur'an in order to become like one of those who is amongst the noble scribes of the angels.

Your Breath
25 | in Prayer

The Prophet (*peace be upon him*) freshened his breath before every meeting with his Lord. Whether he was praying at home or at the mosque, his habit was to brush his teeth with his المِسْوَاك (*al-miswāk*) in preparation for each prayer. Why did he do this? Yet again, the answer lies with the angels. The Messenger of Allah (*peace be upon him*) explained that as a person stands for prayer, an angel stands behind them and listens to their recitation. Then the angel draws near until the mouth of the angel is on the mouth of the reciter and so, 'nothing of the Qur'an comes out of it, but it enters the heart of the angel, إِلَّا صَارَ فِي جَوْفِ المَلَكِ. Therefore, the Prophet advised, فَطَهِّرُوا أَفْوَاهَكُمْ لِلْقُرْآنِ, 'Purify your mouth for the Qur'an'.

Subḥān Allāh! We came into this life with an angel blowing our spirit into us and when we pray, we are blowing the word of Allah into an angel's heart. Ibn al-Salah narrates that angels do not recite the Qur'an, but instead they listen to the recitation, crowding around us in celebration as we recite. Their love for the Qur'an is such, that they surrounded it as it was sent down to the Messenger of Allah (*peace be upon him*). Therefore, when we are readying ourselves for worship we should prepare for the angels, just as we are told to prepare for our fellow worshippers.

Consider the words of the Prophet (*peace be upon him*), 'Whoever amongst you is eating onions or garlic, don't approach the *masjid*'. This is not only to prevent us from distracting others from their prayers with unpleasant odours, but also so as not to offend the angels as the Prophet (*peace be upon him*) tells us that, 'the angels are offended by what offends the children of Adam'. Ensuring our oral hygiene is a small ask when, in return we are pleasing the angels from whom we once absorbed life. *Subḥān Allāh*, the blessings of the Qur'an are so great that even the angel wants to absorb its words from our mouths.

When Jibrīl ﷺ Descends

26

There is no night more beloved to the angels than the night of لَيْلَةُ القَدْرِ, of divine decree. For the angels who rejoice when we recite the Qur'an, spend in charity, make heartfelt supplications to Allah (*glorified and exalted is He*) and gather in congregation with our fellow worshippers, what night could possibly be greater than *Laylat al-Qadr* when people all over the world come together to fast all day, pray all night and give generously in *ṣadaqah*?

The Prophet (*peace be upon him*) said, 'On the night of *Laylat al-Qadr* there are more angels that come to the Earth, than the rocks on it' and one of the signs of *Laylat al-Qadr*, is that the hordes of angels descending on to earth block out the rays of the sun. In fact, it is called لَيْلَةُ القَدْرِ, the Night of Constriction because the angels fill up the heavens as they carry praises to Allah (*glorified and exalted is He*). In Paradise, they enter upon you from every door saying سَلَامٌ عَلَيْكُم بِمَا صَبَرْتُمْ, 'Peace be onto you for the patience that you had', and on earth they visit the mosques and the houses of believers, saying سَلَامٌ، سَلَامٌ، سَلَامٌ, 'peace, peace, peace'. There is nothing that resembles Heaven more than that night, when the people are standing up in admiration and praise of their Lord (*glorified and exalted is He*) and the angels recognise that.

Abū Hurayrah (*Allah's mercy be upon him*) said, 'There are more angels on that night than stars in the galaxy' and amongst them is تَنَزَّلُ الْمَلَائِكَةُ وَالرُّوحُ فِيهَا, Jibrīl. The one who delivered the Qur'an to the Prophet (*peace be upon him*) on the Night of Power comes down on that same night each year in commemoration, but instead of descending upon the Prophet (*peace be upon him*) to reveal the Qur'an, he's descending upon us as we recite it.

Now, consider the *ḥadīth* in which Khadījah (*Allah's mercy be upon her*) was in the home and Jibrīl told

Jibril ﷺ, *the one who delivered the Qur'an to the Prophet* ﷺ *on the Night of Power, comes down on that same night each year in commemoration, but this time, he's descending upon us as we recite it.*

the Prophet (*peace be upon him*) to give her salutation (*Salām*) from her Lord, وَأَقْرِأْهَا مِنِّى السَّلَامَ, and salutation from himself. Whilst none of us can be like the Prophet (*peace be upon him*) who had the Qur'an revealed to him, it could be your home which is graced by the presence, not just of the angels, but of Jibrīl himself. It could be you who Jibrīl visits to convey his *Salām* as he did to Khadījah (*Allah's mercy be upon her*) through the Prophet (*peace be upon him*). Therefore, make your supplications, your recitations and your remembrances worthy of Jibrīl's ears, and more importantly, worthy of your Lord and the Lord of the Worlds (*glorified and exalted is He*) who watches you and hears your prayers on this great night.

The Heavens Are Creaking

27

A NASA study called 'Our Universe Is Not Silent' which captures all of the sounds in outer space, proves that just because space is foreign to us, it does not mean it is still and lifeless. The Prophet (*peace be upon him*) explained that the Heavens are creaking, 'because there is not a span of four fingers except that there is an angel that is standing, bowing, prostrating, and glorifying Allah (*glorified and exalted is He*) in every single space'. To our ears, it may sound almost like chants and shaking, but only Allah (*glorified and exalted is He*) knows how the angels are praising Him and only He (*glorified and exalted is He*) hears the true extent of the Heavens creaking as they expand and more angels are created to fill that space.

We have previously discussed the entourage of angels that accompany you here on earth when you visit the sick or the angels who protect you from the devil when you leave your home with good intentions. Consider then, the following narration in which the Prophet (*peace be upon him*) said, 'When the Imam says *'āmīn'*, then say, *'āmīn'* as well for if your *'āmīn'* coincides with his, it also coincides with the *'āmīn'* of all the angels, meaning Allah (*glorified and exalted is He*) will forgive your previous sins'. Therefore, as you say *'āmīn'*, you are accompanied by the hordes of angels in the ever-expanding Heavens as well as the Imam and your fellow worshippers.

He (*peace be upon him*) added, 'When the Imam says سَمِعَ اللهُ لِمَنْ حَمِدَهُ, Allah has heard the one who has praised Him, and the congregation say رَبَّنَا وَلَكَ الْحَمْدُ, And to you our Lord belongs all praise, the angels utter these words as well and if your words coincide with theirs, your sins will be forgiven'. In other words, it is the entire congregation of Allah (*glorified and exalted is He*) both on earth and in the Heavens who are coming together in unison to worship Him (*glorified and exalted is He*).

In another *ḥadīth*, the Prophet (*peace be upon him*) was leading the Companions (*Allah's mercy be upon them*) in prayer and as he said, سَمِعَ اللهُ لِمَنْ حَمِدَهُ, 'Allah has heard the one that praised Him', he heard a man behind him say, رَبَّنَا وَلَكَ الْحَمْدُ ، حَمْدًا كَثِيرًا طَيِّبًا مُبَارَكًا فِيهِ رَبَّنَا وَلَكَ الْحَمْدُ, to you O Lord belongs all the praise, a praise that is plentiful, حَمْدًا كَثِيرًا, pure, طَيِّبًا, and blessed, مُبَارَكًا فِيهِ. When Allah's Messenger (*peace be upon him*) finished the prayer, he asked, 'Who amongst you said رَبَّنَا وَلَكَ الْحَمْدُ حَمْدًا كَثِيرًا طَيِّبًا مُبَارَكًا فِيهِ رَبَّنَا وَلَكَ الْحَمْدُ' and the Companion (*Allah's mercy be upon them*) answered, 'It was me, O Messenger of Allah'. The Prophet (*peace be upon him*) said, 'I saw thirty angels rushing to catch your praise, so they could have the honour of recording it with Allah (*glorified and exalted is He*)'. Here, we can see how the Prophet's Companion (*Allah's mercy be upon them*) rushes to join him (*peace be upon him*) in his praise of Allah (*glorified and exalted is He*) so that he too may share in the blessings of the angels.

All of the above *aḥādīth* may be different narrations, but they all illustrate the fact that we may count the angels among the congregation we worship in. Remember this when you are next at the mosque.

As you say *'āmīn'* in line with the Imam and as you praise your Lord alongside the person who is leading you in prayer, you are in the company of the multitude of angels in the expanding Heavens and those same angels are rushing to record your praise and deliver it to He who is worthy of all praise (*glorified and exalted is He*).

28 Praying Behind You

We are all aware of what special and blessed spaces our mosques are, but we should also strive to make our homes places of praise for Allah (*glorified and exalted is He*). The Prophet (*peace be upon him*) said, 'Do not turn your homes into graveyards'. We should be mindful of this and always leave a share of our prayers for our houses, even if we attend congregational prayers in the mosque. Our homes, just like the *masjid*, can also be places of blessing (*barakah*) and worship. What better way to expel the devils and Jinn from your home than to invite the angels in with the recitation of Qur'an and the continual presence of prayer and remembrance?

When you make your home a place of worship, you
are never worshipping alone. Of course, Allah
(*glorified and exalted is He*) is ever present, but so too
are the angels. You may not be surrounded by rows of
people as you are at the mosque, but you are still part
of a Heavenly congregation. Saʿīd ibn al-Musayyib
narrates that, 'No one goes into prayer, except that
an angel prays to their right and an angel prays to
their left, and أَمْثَالَ الْجِبَالِ, angels the size of mountains
are praying behind them'. *Subḥān Allāh!* You are
entering into prayer in your bedroom or living room
or wherever else it is, thinking you are alone, when
in fact there are angels the size of mountains that are
praying behind you as you're saying اللهُ أَكْبَر, *Allāhu
akbar.* Armed with this knowledge, will you not recite
with even more sincerity and passion even though no
one else is there?

This sincerity is something which is really emphasised
when we are praying alone and there are two *aḥādīth*
which illustrate this beautifully. The first is from Abū
Saʿīd al-Khudrī who narrates that the Prophet (*peace
be upon him*) said, 'The prayer in congregation is like
twenty-five times the individual prayer and *Ṣalāh* that

is in the wilderness (*falāḥ*) is equivalent to fifty times the reward'. In another *ḥadīth* the Prophet (*peace be upon him*) said:

يُحِبُّ رَبُّكُمْ, Your Lord (*glorified and exalted is He*) is pleased with the shepherd in the mountains all by himself, who calls out the adhan, who does the 'iqama, and performs the prayer all by himself and Allah (*glorified and exalted is He*) calls the angels and says, 'Look at this slave of mine. He does this out of love for me and I have forgiven this servant of mine and I have entered him into Paradise'.

This is the reward for the one who prays with sincerity and clings to Allah (*glorified and exalted is He*) even when they are completely isolated. This may be in the middle of the wilderness or it may be alone in your bedroom, but your sincerity and your dedication to your Lord (*glorified and exalted is He*) even when others are not there to witness or encourage you is rewarded generously by Allah (*glorified and exalted is He*) with the promise of Paradise and the company of the angels who surround you as you pray.

*No one goes
into prayer, except that
an angel prays to their
right and an angel
prays to their left,
and angels the size
of mountains are
praying behind them.*

29 Gatherings of Remembrance

The remembrance of Allah (*glorified and exalted is He*) when alone, and the remembrance of Allah (*glorified and exalted is He*) within a gathering, both possess their own unique benefits. When you are sitting in isolation and remembering Allah (*glorified and exalted is He*), the angels will surely accompany you and that will not compromise your intention, but only increase your sincerity. When you are sitting with others and remembering Allah (*glorified and exalted is He*), that will increase the number of angels present and cause the mercy of Allah (*glorified and exalted is He*) to descend on every single person in that gathering.

In a Ḥadīth Qudsī, Allah (*glorified and exalted is He*)
says, 'I am as my servant expects of Me, and I am
with him when he remembers Me. So if he remembers
Me inwardly, I remember him inwardly, and if he
remembers Me in an assembly, I remember him in
a greater assembly', meaning the assembly of the
angels. This explains the blessing that accompanies
the different types of remembrance and why it is
important to have a share of each.

The rewards for those who come together to remember
their Lord (*glorified and exalted is He*) are not restricted
to a particular type of remembrance, a specific
location or number of people. The Prophet (*peace be
upon him*) said:

The angels are traversing the streets every single night
looking for people that are gathered in remembrance
of Allah (*glorified and exalted is He*) and when those
angels come across those groups of people, they call
upon the others and say, هَلُمُّوا إِلَى حَاجَتِكُم, 'We have
found what you were looking for. Join us'. Then they
all extend their wings over that gathering and as they
extend their wings all the way up to the Heavens,

they are stacked on top of one another and Allah (*glorified and exalted is He*), although He knows us better than the angels do, asks them, 'Why are these people gathered?' to which the angels reply, 'They are gathered to remember You', and Allah (*glorified and exalted is He*) asks, 'What are they saying?' and the angels reply, سُبْحَانَ اللهِ، وَالْحَمْدُ لِلَّهِ، وَلَا إِلَهَ إِلَّا اللَّهُ، وَاللَّهُ أَكْبَرُ, 'They are remembering You, they are glorifying You and they are learning about You' and Allah (*glorified and exalted is He*) asks, 'What are they asking?' and the angels tell Him 'They are asking for Heaven…and for refuge from the Fire'…and Allah (*glorified and exalted is He*) responds, 'I want you all to bear witness that I have forgiven all of these people'.

The Prophet (*peace be upon him*) explained how the angels tell Allah (*glorified and exalted is He*) that one of those people is there for some reason other than the sincere remembrance of their Lord, whether it is for the social element of such occasions or because they were pressured by their friends to attend and Allah's response is, لَا يَشْقَى بِهِمْ جَلِيسُهُمْ, 'The one who sits amongst this group of people will not be deprived'. This shows that the mercy of Allah (*glorified and exalted is He*) is such, that just by being present at such a gathering, your sins will be forgiven.

The blessings available to those who attend such gatherings cannot be over-emphasised. The Prophet (*peace be upon him*) said, 'The angels surround them, mercy overtakes them, tranquillity descends upon them and Allah (*glorified and exalted is He*) praises them to the angels'. Although there is no issue with accessing and consuming Islamic knowledge online, it does not compare to learning and worshipping together in the company of the angels. Therefore, we should seek out gatherings of remembrance whenever the opportunity arises, even if it is only locally or with a minimal number of people. Seek out the blessings of the angels, the praise and forgiveness of Allah (*glorified and exalted is He*) and the tranquillity of heart that His Messenger (*peace be upon him*) promises.

When Allah Loves You

Too often we equate fame with the love of Allah (*glorified and exalted is He*) when in fact, it could be that a person walks this earth unknown to people but loved by Allah (*glorified and exalted is He*) and the angels. This does not mean they will remain unloved in this world. All real love stems from the love of Allah (*glorified and exalted is He*) and it is His love alone, that we should seek unconditionally. The Prophet (*peace be upon him*) said, 'Verily if Allah (*glorified and exalted is He*) loves someone, إِنَّ اللهَ إِذَا أَحَبَّ عَبْدًا نَادَى جِبْرِيل He (*glorified and exalted is He*) calls Jibrīl and says يَا جِبْرِيل، إِنِّى أُحِبُّ فُلَانًا, "O Jibrīl, I want you to know that I love this person, so you should love this person also". Jibrīl needs only the knowledge that you are loved by your Lord (*glorified and exalted is He*) to love you, فَيُحِبُّهُ جِبْرِيلُ, so Jibrīl loves you as well. Then Jibrīl calls all of the angels and he says, إِنَّ اللهَ يُحِبُّ فُلَانًا, to the inhabitants of the Heavens, "Allah loves this person so love them too". Therefore, all those who abide in the Heavens love that person as well'. The Prophet (*peace be upon him*) concluded, 'Allah (*glorified and exalted is He*) mentions, يُوضَعُ لَهُ الْقَبُولُ فِي الْأَرْضِ and acceptance is then placed in the hearts of the people for that person'.

Strive to gain the love of Allah (*glorified and exalted is He*) and anyone whose love is worth having will follow. If your Lord (*glorified and exalted is He*) loves you, the angels will love you, and the people in this world whose love is worth having will love you as well. It is only logical that the love that originates from Allah (*glorified and exalted is He*) shows itself amongst the righteous people who love you for your righteousness. As Ibn al-Jawzī (*May Allah be pleased with him*) said 'If people are impressed by you, know that they are impressed by the hijab, the cover that Allah (*glorified and exalted is He*) has given you because they don't really know you' and the reality is that people have to love you for a righteousness that is actually true of you, not merely what is on the surface.

In other words, the people who are beloved to Allah (*glorified and exalted is He*) حُبُّ مَنْ يُحِبُّكَ, 'The love of those that love You', is transferred to you as well and when Allah (*glorified and exalted is He*) loves you, all that is good of His creation loves you including His angels. The value of Allah's creation is only to the extent that it brings you closer to the Creator, and that is true even of His angels. May Allah (*glorified and exalted is He*) make us beloved to Him, make us beloved to Jibrīl, make us beloved to the angels, make us beloved to the Prophet (*peace be upon him*) and to all of those righteous people who follow the Prophet (*peace be upon him*). May Allah (*glorified and exalted is He*) gather us in that station of love in the presence of the beloved (*peace be upon him*) in the highest ranks of Paradise where the angels will enter upon us regularly to wish us 'peace' and we can behold the glory of our Lord (*glorified and exalted is He*) day and night.

May Allah

make us beloved to Him, to Jibrīl ﷺ, to the angels, to the Prophet ﷺ and to all of the righteous people who follow the Prophet ﷺ. Āmīn.

~ Notes ~

～ Notes ～